The
Connell Guide
to
Shakespeare's

King Lear

by
Valentine
Cunningham

Contents

Introduction   4

A note on the text   7

A summary of the plot   7

What is *King Lear* about?   18

What is it that breaks down in *Lear*?   29

How important are the gods?   40

So how Christian is *Lear*?   46

What do we make of Bedlam Tom's
gibberish?   58

Why is Edgar so important?   62

To what extent is Nature being
questioned?   78

How does Shakespeare show us a world
reduced to "nothing"?   81

Does the play undermine language
itself?   85

How sympathetic is Shakespeare's
treatment of women in *Lear*?   92

Where does *Lear* leave us in the end?   107

So how does *Lear* look forward to
Beckett and the Theatre of the
Absurd?   112

NOTES
───────

Shakespeare's sources   22
The vileness of Regan   35
"I am your host"   36
The Fool   41
Lear *and Holy Communion*   54
Samuel Harsnett   59
Letters in Lear   66
Ten facts about King Lear   68
Human animals   74
A tragedy of language   85
Hysterica passio   94
The critics on Lear   104
A short chronology   122
The different versions of King Lear   124
Bibliography   128

Introduction

Lear is too much. There's too much to stomach, an overdoing of massive wickednesses which rightly provoked perhaps the most famous reaction to *King Lear* ever, Dr Samuel Johnson's horror in his Prefaces to his *Shakespeare* (1765) over the blinding of Gloucester –"an act too horrid to be endured in dramatick exhibition" – and the death of Cordelia: "contrary to the natural ideas of justice, to the hope of the reader, and, what is yet more strange, to the faith of the chronicles".

There are indeed just too many awful enhancements of the Lear stories Shakespeare drew on, a superfluity of terrible things – and of course these are uneasily central to a play which teaches the immorality of the well-off having a "superflux" of money and things when the poor have so little (III.iv.35: *superflux* is a Shakespeare coinage); in which frustrations over losing the "addition" (I.i.137) of a king help dement Lear; and where he is driven to strip off his rich man's excess of clothing in sympathy with the nakedness of Edgar and of all "unaccommodated men".

This is irony indeed, you might think, in a play gravely overburdened with Shakespeare's many plot additions, his busy borrowing from all over, his own superflux of textual stuff. And there are so many things that they need a kind of gabbling to cram them into the drama's few allowed hours on stage. Everything, from Lear's shockingly hasty turning against Cordelia onwards – Kent banished, the King of France departing in anger, Lear departing for Goneril's place – occurs, as Gloucester puts it of the play's rapidly spinning opening moves, "upon the gad" (I.ii.23-6): all hurriedly, like an animal goaded with a metal spike or gad; on the rapid move, the gad; gaddingly.

And it's an abrupt pile-up, or switchback, of events which leaves little space anywhere for examination, explanation, motivation – the kind of extended analysis of character and motives, the inspection of decision-making, which would become normal in 19th-century classic realist fiction, in the novels of George Eliot, say, or Leo Tolstoy. An overall thinness of explanation which greatly disappointed A.C. Bradley, the most influential of all commentators on Shakespeare's tragedies, in his *Shakespearian Tragedy: Lectures on Hamlet, Othello, King Lear, Macbeth* (1904, and in print ever since).

And yet, Bradley conceded, this play was the "fullest revelation of Shakespeare's power" – up there with Aeschylus's *Prometheus Bound*, Dante's *Divine Comedy*, Beethoven's symphonies and Michelangelo's statues; the most moving and daunting of tragic experiences the world has ever known promoted by a greatly trashy plot, or, as the poet and critic D. J. Enright puts in his lively book about teaching Shakespeare, *Shakespeare and the*

Students (1970): "It is possible that Shakespeare never did anything more awe-inspiring, more improbable-seeming than this – to take a petulant old retired monarch, drive him mad and stick flowers in his hair, and still end with a figure of tragedy."

THE CHARACTERS

LEAR
GONERIL, *Lear's eldest daughter*
REGAN, *Lear's second daughter*
CORDELIA, *Lear's youngest daughter*
DUKE OF ALBANY, *husband to Goneril*
DUKE OF CORNWALL, *husband to Regan*
EARL OF GLOUCESTER
EARL OF KENT
EDGAR, *Gloucester's son*
EDMUND, *Gloucester's illegitimate son*
OSWALD, *steward to Goneril*
FOOL
KING OF FRANCE, *suitor to Cordelia*
DUKE OF BURGUNDY, *suitor to Cordelia*
CURAN, *a courtier*
Old man, Tenant of Gloucester, A Doctor, an Officer employed by Edmund, a Gentleman attending on Cordelia, a Herald, Servants to Cornwall, Knights of Lear's Train, Officers, Messengers, Soldiers, and Attendants

A note on the text

The text of *King Lear* has caused more arguments than the text of any other Shakespeare play. The standard *King Lear* of modern times – and the one mainly used in this volume – is the version in the handiest modern edition of *King Lear*, edited by R.A. Foakes for the 3rd series of the Arden Shakespeares (1997). In the usual modern way Foakes's text is basically *The Tragedie of King Lear* as it appeared in the expensive Folio collection of Shakespeare's plays (big books, known in the critical trade as F) published by a pair of Shakespeare's fellow-actors John Heminges and Henry Condell in December 1623, seven years after Shakespeare's death, with some prominent bits of the earlier 1608 cheapo Quarto version (half the size of F and known as Q), the *True Chronicle Historie of the life and death of King Lear and his three Daughters*, thrown in. There are many differences between Q and F. For a full discussion of these, see p.124.

A summary of the plot

ACT I. scene i Scene: a royal palace, somewhere in ancient Britain. The aged Duke of Gloucester comes on with his bastard son Edmund, just returned from nine years away somewhere, boasting to King Lear's faithful courtier Kent about how good the sex was in his fathering the foxy young man. This is the short prelude to old and would-be valetudinarian Lear's theatrical test on his two older daughters, Goneril and Regan (married to the Dukes Albany and Cornwall) and the as yet unmarried young Cordelia. Dividing up his kingdom, the King says he'll give the largest portion to the daughter with the amplest declaration of absolute love for her father (though clearly he's fixed the gifting quantities in advance: Coleridge famously labelled the whole show a "trick").

Cannily greedy, Goneril and Regan play ball effusively and get their shares. Cordelia, daddy's favourite, and in line for the meatiest portion, won't play their hypocritical game – how could she love her father more than the husband she hopes for? She will say nothing that her father wants to hear and so gets nothing but a disowning curse from the peeved Lear. The other sisters share Cordelia's destined handout. Staunch Kent is banished with hateful words from Lear for daring to protest. One of Cordelia's suitors, the King of Burgundy, turns her down now she's penniless; the other, the King of France, admiring her "virtue", will take her as his queen. She leaves for France with prophetic words about trouble in store at the hands of the newly empowered daughters. Rather shocked by Lear's ill-treatment of Cordelia and Kent, they mutter conspiratorially about how they'll have to control his "unruly waywardness" when he stays with them, as he plans to do.

I.ii Edmund, annoyed at being a "bastard" – the "natural" but illegitimate son – uses a letter he's forged, to trick Gloucester into believing his legitimate son Edgar wants to kill his father and thus come straightaway into his inheritance. Gloucester blames recent eclipses of sun and moon for such a breakdown in the natural relations between father and son; Edmund, cynical about astrology, knows it's not the stars that make crooks, liars, drunkards and adulterers but human nature. He'll be your naturally bad man – a bastard in the modern colloquial sense. He easily cons his brother Edgar into believing his life is threatened by an angry father.

I.iii Goneril, enraged at the rowdy behaviour of her father's 100 knights, lodging at her place in the first of Lear's planned stays with his older daughters, orders her Steward Oswald to be rude and unhelpful so as to incite Lear and his gang into going off to sister Regan's.

I.iv The banished Kent, in disguise, offers his services to Lear, proving instantly useful in insulting, tripping up and pushing out the insulting Oswald. Lear's Fool does his normal professional job as awkward, goading, truth-telling commentator on the mess Lear has got himself into. Goneril and Lear quarrel bitterly over Lear's rumbustious mob of knights and squires; he must cut it down to 50 men. Lear, enraged, berating himself for foolishness, curses her as a "thankless child" and wishes childlessness on her. Albany urges patience on Lear, but also starts to show concern at Goneril's behaviour. Goneril sends Oswald with a warning letter to sister Regan, and lays into Albany for showing undue kindness towards Lear.

I.v Unaware of Goneril's correspondence with Regan, Lear heads off with his men to Regan's place, sending Kent on ahead with letters for Gloucester.

ACT II. scene i Edmund is the recipient of gossip about possible dissension between Cornwall and Albany. He persuades Edgar to flee for his life, and, pretending his self-inflicted sword-cuts came from his alleged father-hating brother, has Gloucester organise a hue and cry. Cornwall commends Edmund as a good son and takes him into his employment.

II.ii Arriving disguised at Regan's place with those letters from Lear, Kent picks a fight with Goneril's postman Oswald, beats him up and is put in the stocks as punishment by Cornwall, with Regan cruelly upping the duration of the sentence – let him stay there all night! Kent reads a letter from Cordelia about seeking remedies for what's going on.

II.iii Edgar, escaped from his pursuers, purposes to go around in disguise as a ragged, filthied-up, mad tramp called "poor Tom", begging for a living with lunatic shouts and prayers.

II.iv Lear's anger at finding his man Kent in the stocks turns into mounting hysteria as Kent puts all the blame on Regan and Cornwall. These two refuse to meet Lear and then, Goneril having arrived, she and Regan beat down to five, and then none, the number of Lear's allowed entourage. "What need one?" is Regan's final contribution – so much for the better treatment Lear looked forward to from her. More and more demented at his girls' hostility, vowing vengeance on "you unnatural hags", Lear storms off into the terribly stormy night. Contemptuously, the women and Cornwall scorn Gloucester's concern about Lear being outside in such bad weather and lock their doors.

ACT III. scene i Out in the storm, searching for Lear, Kent (still disguised) dispatches one of Lear's knights to Dover to report to Cordelia "how unnatural and bemadding sorrow" is afflicting the ex-king.

III.ii Raving ("My wits begin to turn"), Lear invokes the thunderstorm to beat down on his old head like his "two pernicious" daughters, while his Fool, joined by Kent, urges him to take shelter in a "hovel".

III.iii Gloucester complains to Edmund about Lear's unnatural treatment. Against the orders of Cornwall and co. he'll go and look for Lear. It's time to take sides with the forces already afoot on the ex-king's side. Unaware of Edmund's allegiance to Cornwall, Gloucester asks his son to cover for him with Cornwall – who has threatened to kill Gloucester should he try to help Lear.

III.iv Lear – a "tempest" in his mind now more tormenting than the one beating physically down on him – is driven to think, for the first time ever, of the plight of the "poor naked wretches" of his kingdom. Edgar, posing as Poor Tom, emerges naked from the hovel gibbering with calculated zaniness about poverty, the devil, sexually bad women, corruption in high places. Lear thinks only bad daughters could have brought him to such a pitch of distress. Gloucester advises Kent that Lear can't be blamed for "unsettled wits": his daughters mean to kill him. Grief over his own beloved son's plotting to kill his father has "crazed" his own wits. Small wonder the utterances of Poor Tom sound utterly crazy: "Childe Rowland to the dark tower came". Gloucester and Kent at last push Lear into the hovel. "No words, no words, hush," urges Gloucester.

III.v Edmund shows Cornwall a letter revealing that Gloucester is conniving with France (and Cordelia) against Cornwall and the rest. Cornwall commissions Edmund to help capture his father. Edmund is Earl of Gloucester now – truly illegitimate heir to the title legitimate Edgar would expect.

III.vi Raving, but with attitude and point, and urged on by the Fool's cryptic wisdoms about madness, Lear arraigns his daughters in a mock trial, with Poor Tom and the Fool as the learned judges. Regan must be "anatomized". Lear's question for the judges: "Is there any cause in nature that makes these hard hearts?" Gloucester urges Kent to take Lear away to safety in Dover. Edgar draws a parallel between his fate and Lear's: "He childed as I fathered" – two men cast out by their own families.

III.vii Cornwall spares Edmund from seeing what he and Regan plan to do with "traitorous" Gloucester, by sending him to Albany along with Goneril, she bearing letters about the French invasion. The awful couple tie the old man to a chair, so Cornwall can more easily gouge out one of his eyes. Regan urges him to do the other one. A servant intervenes, stabbing Cornwall, but is killed with a sword-stroke from Regan. Cornwall gouges out the other eye. Eyeless, Gloucester wishes Edmund were here to revenge "this horrid act". Regan gleefully informs him Edmund betrayed Gloucester to them. It dawns on him that Edgar's been abused; he begs the gods' forgiveness. Regan throws him out: he can "smell /His way to Dover". Cornwall exits, badly hurt. Some kindly servants will wipe Gloucester's bleeding eyesockets with soothing eggwhites.

ACT IV. scene i Edgar, still in Poor Tom disguise, meets blinded Gloucester on the road being led by an old man. Gloucester gives this raving beggar money to lead him to Dover: "'Tis the time's plague when madmen lead the blind".

IV.ii Goneril comes on to Edmund, so much more attractively a tough guy than her husband Albany, who's going all soft in the matter of Lear's treatment. Albany, shocked at the news of Gloucester's blinding, is glad to hear of Cornwall's mortal wounding by the servant, and vows revenge on Gloucester's torturers.

IV.iii A Gentleman brings news to Kent of the French King's sudden return to France, of Cordelia's distress on hearing of Lear's ordeal in the storm, and of the assembling of Albany's and Cordelia's forces.

IV.iv Cordelia sends people to find Lear who's been reported going about utterly mad, singing, crowned with wild flowers and weeds. Her troops are ready for the "British powers": she's on her own now, as military commander.

IV.v Regan tells Oswald it was a mistake to let Gloucester live. Fancying Edmund for herself, she wheedles Goneril's letter to him off Oswald, substituting one of her own. On the promise of a substantial reward, Oswald enthusiastically takes on Regan's commission to murder Gloucester.

IV.vi Now disguised as a peasant, Edgar pretends to lead Gloucester to the cliffs of Dover where he wants to jump to his death. Edgar paints a rhapsodic picture of this fearful place, and Gloucester, deceived, throws himself forward onto level ground. Doing yet one more voice, Edgar assures Gloucester that he has miraculously survived. Lear turns up, completely mad, crowned with wild flowers; takes Gloucester for Goneril in a white beard; urges him to see "with his ears" the upside-down way of the world in which judges are the offenders and the rich get away with great crimes. This is "Reason in madness", Edgar thinks. A "ruined piece of nature", reduced to "nought", in

Gloucester's words, Lear laments, pathetically, his being born (sounding much like Old Testament Job); rages violently against his sons-in-law; and runs off, evading Cordelia's people who have come to help him. Oswald appears, attempts to murder Gloucester and is chopped down by Edgar, who is posing, much to hoity-toity Oswald's vexation, as a peasant. Edgar opens Goneril's letter that Oswald was carrying, urging Edmund to kill her husband Albany, with her body as the reward.

IV.vii Cordelia is reunited with Lear. He's astonished she doesn't hate him; she's moved at her old father's not being in "perfect mind". Kent prepares for battle with the forces of the dead Cornwall, now led by Edmund.

ACT V. scene 1 Regan and Goneril jostle over Edmund. Edgar, in peasant role, involves a mystified Albany in his plan to get Edmund. Edmund soliloquises about which sister he'll "take", and how Albany must be forestalled in showing mercy to Lear and Cordelia.

V.ii Battle is raging. Edgar and Gloucester reflect briefly on the need for stoicism in life.

V.iii Edmund has taken Lear and Cordelia prisoner. Lear fantasises about a happy loving future in prison with his daughter – reminiscing, praying, singing, laughing, jeering at the worlds of court and power. Edmund gives a Captain written orders to bump off Lear and Cordelia. Albany gets in the way of Edmund's plans for supremacy and of Goneril's and Regan's hots for Edmund. Regan feels the effects of the poison Goneril has slipped her. Edgar appears, masked, upon the trumpet-calls fixed up with Albany; challenges Edmund as a "manifold traitor"; mortally wounds him; narrates the tale of how Poor Tom saved Gloucester from despair and reports that Gloucester died happy just now upon hearing that story. A Gentleman reports that Goneril has stabbed herself to death.

Moved by Edgar's story and by thoughts of two women's love for him, Edmund owns up to his and Goneril's scheme to have Cordelia hanged in prison. As messengers scurry off to prevent this, Lear enters carrying the dead Cordelia. He holds a mirror up to her mouth to see if she is still breathing. He claims to have killed "the slave" who was hanging her. He wonders who Kent is. Albany dismisses a report that Edmund is dead as "but a trifle here". Lear asks why a dog, a horse, a rat should have life and Cordelia no breath at all. "And my poor fool is hanged", the now dying Lear says. Cordelia will "come no more", Lear wails: "Never, never, never, never, never". And he dies commanding "Look on her: Look, her lips, / Look there, look there!" Does he think she is still alive? Albany, now in charge, assigns rule and order to

Kent and Edgar. Kent passes on the offer, mystifyingly declaring he has a journey to go on: "My master calls me". Who's that, and is this a suicide note? Edgar has the play's last word – about obeying "The weight of this sad time": "we that are young/ shall never see so much, nor live so long". And the surviving few – Albany, Kent, Edgar – troop off the stage to a dead march.

What is *King Lear* about?

What a plot! Nothing quite like it in all of world literature. A very wild thing, certainly not at all constrained by Aristotle's 2,300-year-old (or so) *Poetics* with its "model" for tragedies, dramas ruled by the "unities" of time and place and action, whose heroes go through a standard process of hubristic rise and catastrophic fall – "rules" Shakespeare had probably never heard of, and even if he had he was ignoring (which hasn't stopped critics repeatedly invoking them). Of course Shakespeare didn't invent *Lear's* core elements. In his usual way, he plundered previous stories, previous texts. A love-test involving a father and three daughters is one of the oldest of European folktale motifs, and versions of it involving a mythical British king Leyr and his three daughters, Gonorilla, Regan and Cordeilla, were all over the place in Shakespeare's time.

But Shakespeare's tinkering with the core

elements was dramatically extensive. His Lear dies in the end, unlike in all the preceding versions, in which he's restored to the throne with the help of Cordelia, who succeeds him as Queen when he eventually dies. No sisters die in the *King Leir* play of 1605, which is based on old accounts: all three die in *Lear*, including Cordelia, so shockingly hanged on Edmund's command. In the 1605 *Leir* the Kent figure is not banished, doesn't spend time in disguise, and is finally rewarded for loyalty (see Shakespeare's Sources, p.22-3).

With such tinkerings Shakespeare made his version so much more daunting, so much more morbidly bleak than its predecessors – so much more tragic, as the whole history of the varied thoughts about what "tragedy" is would put it. He thickened his play's darknesses quite dauntingly. As Edgar says (IV.i.27-30), you think the worst has happened, but, no, there's always something worse to come. Lear's dementia; the blinding of Gloucester; the storm scene of Act III; Poor Tom's ravings (worked up out of Samuel Harsnett's recent Protestant attack on fake Jesuit exorcisms, *A Declaration of Egregious Popishe Impostures* (1603), involving a crooked priest called Edmunds, who might well have given his blackened name to Shakespeare's Edmund); the haunting echoes in Lear's mental and physical degradation of the sufferings of Job in the Old Testament; Goneril's evil henchman Oswald; the Fool, a constant

endorser and reminder of the play's worstnesses –
these are all Shakespeare's add-ons.

The add-ons keep on remorselessly extending
the play's dementing pile-up of terrible events.
Troubles in this play keep on doubling.
Shakespeare's largest add-on – the so-called
Double Plot in which the case of old Gloucester,
molested through the evil of his son Edmund at the
expense of good son Edgar – horribly mirrors old
Lear's plight as he misjudges his good daughter and
falls into the hands of his bad ones. It's a terrible
pairing affirmed as Gloucester finds insight
through blindness and Lear sanity in madness
in the play's twinned key moral provocations.

Shakespeare lifted the Gloucester plot from
Philip Sidney's assembly of violent stories in
relishing prose in the *Arcadia* (II.10), where he'd
found the awful tale of an old king of Paphlagonia,
incited by his bastard son to hate and outlaw his
legitimate one. Deposed, blinded and driven out
by the unnaturally unkind bastard, this king is
encountered, weather-beaten, poorly clothed,
being led up a high rocky place by his amazingly
forgiving and kind legitimate son who is, though,
refusing to let his father throw himself over the
edge to his death: terrible fictional grist to the
Lear mill which Shakespeare just couldn't resist
working in. The effect of his ghastly additions – the
utter evil of Edmund, the blinding of Gloucester –
is not at all mitigated by the kindness of Edgar.

Nigel Hawthorne as King Lear in a 1999 RSC production directed by Yukio Ninagawa. He said of his performance: "One advantage of doing Lear at 70 is that you don't have to play an old man."

They contribute mightily to the sense of sheer gothic excess which pervades this play.

It's all too much, and too quick. "Character is destiny," is Bradley's principle for a convincing fiction. He got it from George Eliot, who got it from the German Romantic philosopher "Novalis", and he thinks that the destinies, the lives, of this play's significant people aren't convincing because no time is taken to provide – indeed no interest is shown in supplying – the plausible back-stories, logics, rationales a George Eliot would give us in plenty. "Shakespeare has too vast a material to use

SHAKESPEARE'S SOURCES

It's pretty unlikely that Shakespeare read Geoffrey of Monmouth's fabled 12th-century Latin *History of the Kingdom of Britain*. But he was familiar with the poetic "tragedy" of Cordila in Henry Higgins's edition of the *Mirour for Magistrates* (1574), based on Geoffrey's version. His favourite English history book, Raphael Holinshed's *Chronicles of England, Scotland and Ireland* (1577), included the story, as did Edmund Spenser's epic poem *The Fairie Queene* (1590) in a Chronicle of British kings in Book II, Canto X, which Shakespeare also read.

Even more suggestive for Shakespeare was the anonymous play about Lear and his daughters performed by the Queen's Men at the Rose Theatre in April 1594, and which Shakespeare actually acted in. This sentimental tragi-comedy was registered for publication twice in 1605,

with complete dramatic effectiveness." There's so much, and so much failing to add up. Lear's "improbabilities, inconsistencies, sayings and doings which suggest questions only to be answered by conjecture" are more numerous and "grosser" than in any other Shakespearian tragedy.

Bradley piles on the offensive detail. Why is Gloucester so foolish as to believe Edgar might have written a letter to his brother living in the same house instead of speaking to him – a letter, what's more, incriminating himself? Why did Edgar run away without asking Gloucester why

first as *The Most Famous Chronicle history of Leire King of England his three Daughters Gonorill, Ragan and Cordilla,* then as *The Tragicall historie of King Leir and his three Daughters....*

Intriguingly, too, there were some newsworthy contemporary legal struggles involving Brian Annesley, a wealthy Kentish Gentleman, a former functionary of Henry VIII, who had three daughters, Grace, Christian and his youngest, Cordell. In 1600 old Annesley bequeathed the bulk of his estate to Cordell. In October 1603 Grace's husband tried to take over her father's estate on grounds of mental incapacity, which Cordell successfully opposed with the help of a friend in high places, Robert Cecil. When Annesley died a few months later Grace disputed the Will, but the courts upheld Cordell's rights.

Some literary historians think it was cashing in on the Annesley case which prompted the publication in 1605 of the old *Leir* play, and stimulated Shakespeare's interest in recasting the Lear and daughters story for his own part as a Chronicle History-cum-Tragedy ■

he is being reported angry? Why should Lear and Goneril send letters to Regan asking the messengers to hurry back with replies when both of them are hastening en route to Regan? Why should Gloucester "wander painfully all the way to Dover in order to destroy himself"? Why doesn't Edgar reveal himself to his blind father? What's the point of Kent preserving his "incognito" almost to the very end? Why does Edmund delay in trying to save his victims? And so on and on – so much uninspected action, so many holes and improbabilities; incredibility everywhere, and right at the core of things.

The extremely important paralleled relationships between Lear and his daughters and Gloucester and his sons are, Bradley gnashes, "arbitrary and do not flow from the characters or the natural course of events". The play is full of untidinesses, even daftnesses, which Bradley's admired realistic novels would never have allowed. No wonder old Leo Tolstoy jeered at great length at the play's unnaturalness and improbability. Tolstoy can't believe that Lear, "however old and stupid", should believe his "vicious" daughters, whom he's known all his life, and turn so viciously against his beloved Cordelia. Lear's rant and cursings are all "strange and unnatural". Gloucester's relations with his sons defy belief. Just because Shakespeare had recently read Samuel Harsnett's book there was no reason to give Edgar so many of Harsnett's words. So much of the Fool stuff is just bad jokes; Lear's "awful ravings" are as embarrassing as bad jokes are. Too many speeches of Lear and Gloucester have no rationale or meaning except as driven by mere wordplay – "characteristic Shakespearian language", which Tolstoy was, of course, sharp in spotting.

Why, Tolstoy sneers, does Lear go around "covered with wild flowers"? The final scenes, involving the Edmund challenge, Edgar's long life-stories, and then all the killings, are for him absurd. Lear's a sick man more than 80 years old, so how come he can carry in the dead Cordelia? And so on: the play's "insanity, murders, plucking out of eyes, Gloucester's jump, its poisonings, and wranglings: all absurd. Shakespeare does not satisfy the most elementary demands of art recognised by all."

Tolstoy was ranting, of course. George Orwell astutely suggested Tolstoy's hostility was fired by discomfiting parallels with Lear: an angry old aristocrat who freed his serfs on anarcho-pacifist-religious grounds, but couldn't give up his aristocratic ways and ended up horribly disappointed with his life. Orwell had to agree about excessive length: "too many characters and sub-plots", one too many wicked daughters, and no need for Gloucester and his sons. But, unlike Tolstoy, and like Bradley, he was compelled to concede that this absurdly operatic mess of often silly overdoings had overwhelming impact on readers and playgoers.

Some of the difficulty of making sense of the play arises from the pretence that *Lear* is a single literary entity. The pretence has long been endorsed by the traditional practice – continued on principle by R.A. Foakes's latest Arden text – of giving us a blatantly conflated text, based on the 1623 folio text of *The Tragedie of King Lear* (F), with selected bits and variants from the earlier 1608 version (Q), plus selected emendations taken from the long history of serious editions, especially in the 18th century.

The result is a textual plethora, often an actual contradictoriness, an essential and important textual multi-irresoluteness which doesn't strike the audience in the theatre, but is pretty plain to the reader of an edited text, with its array of footnotes, textual variants, and indications of different F and Q readings. This important fact brings us close to the old feeling that *Lear* has difficulty succeeding on stage and is actually better consumed, book in hand, like a novel or a long poem.

Critic after critic has been despondent about *Lear* working on stage: Charles Lamb, for example ("essentially impossible to represent on stage"), or Henry James ("impossible to imagine a drama that accommodates itself less to the stage"). L.C. Knights thought "the only possible approach" was to consider *Lear* and other great Shakespeare tragedies as "dramatic poems". A.C. Bradley was certain *Lear* was better read than seen.

The irresoluteness of the play is evident in its extreme habit of raising questions which don't get answered, so many of them questions of the largest existential, ethical, political, philosophical and religious kind.* What's goodness? Why evil; why suffering? What's a just society like? Is the cosmos meaningless? What price moral redemption? Is God allowing evil and suffering? How far are human beings responsible for their behaviour? And the play won't tell. Crucially it asks: can you tell the difference between the good person and the bad, insight and blindness, sanity and madness? Poison: medicine (see the discussion of verbal differences, pages 125-6), which is which?

In other words – key ones in the play – Lear is playing a dramatic game of *handy-dandy*. Ranting on to Gloucester about what can be seen with no eyes, Lear gets round to the way law officers are in fact indistinguishable from criminals: "change places and handy-dandy, which is the justice, which is the thief?" (IV.vi). Handy-dandy: a kiddy game of choice – which hand is an object hidden

---

*The number of questions in the play was one of the things which struck the actor Brian Cox as he prepared to play the title role in Deborah Warner's 1990 National Theatre production. "One of the things I discovered today was how many questions [Lear] asks," he noted in his diary.

in? The player chooses which is which. And in this play you, the audience, have to decide. Morally, politically, socially, the play is tauntingly indecisive – it won't tell you what to conclude about the great issues it raises. Here certainties are refused, questions held open, judgements waived. And this profoundly unsettling irresoluteness is rooted in the persistent unfixity of the textual vehicle which productions, in their need for certainties, have to resist. Theatre directors are compelled to decide between the variances and differences of Q and F. Only readers of the play realise what should, of course, be realised, namely the mess of *Lear*, its utter splitness, the dividedness which editors have long had to deal with.

For this is a divided text all right, full of contradictions, and the divided text underlines the dividedness at the very heart of this play; it is there in all aspects of it. Simply everything follows from Lear's genetic act of breaking up his country, his division of his kingdom. "Now... the division of the Kingdom" are almost the first words we hear. "There is division," says Kent of the building conflict between Albany and Cornwall (III.i.19). There is division full stop. It's what this play is about.

What is it that breaks down in *Lear*?

Monarchs were supposed to unite not divide the people, their country. The tearing, cutting, scrunching of the map with which productions often begin bring home the awful violence to selves and nation that Lear is initiating. Lear's descent into breakdown, his mental disintegration, begins in that luridly theatrical dividing up of his physical properties. Property, the things you own, and your properties of character, what you are: the verbal equation brings home their intimate linkage in the history and imagination of western bourgeois culture. That men are equated with what they own is massively indicated in this play by the men named for land and lands, men as a species of geography, bits of map, who cram the opening stage – Gloucester, Kent, Cornwall, Albany, France, Burgundy. Break up the one sort and the other sort is always in danger of crack-up. And so it is with Lear, and with those around him.

The speedy exile of Kent, Lear's first critic, quickly followed by France's exit with Cordelia, are the first indicators of the general crack-up Lear has started: people at odds, regional break-up, civil war, war between France and England. Personal breakdown and geographical crack-up intersect. The land, the map, and the people on it – people as mappable entities – all come to pieces. The great resonance of Dover – the only actual place featured as such – England's border with France, the risky emotive edge of personal and national identity, the gateway by which the banished exit and the enemy might arrive – underlines the story here of national and personal trauma. Dover is, of course, in Kent.

What breaks down in *Lear* is mutual obligation, and the tragedy is the awful consequence, the evil, which results from that breakdown, the smash-up of the ties which bind or should bind every social set from the smallest family unit to the largest group, a whole kingdom. In Shakespeare's time, every possible relationship, between parents and children, husbands and wives, siblings, masters and servants, guests and hosts, priest and parishioner, the citizen and the ruling powers (magistrates, kings and queens, God), carried its sense of mutual obligation: what ought to be, and to be done; what was owed by each party in every relationship. Sometimes it was codified in writing, in sermons, legal documents, contracts, and so forth; sometimes it was just the behaviour everybody knew was due because implicit in custom and everyday practice; what was felt, indeed, as simply natural.

The Elizabethan Prayer Book is packed with such mutualities: every person is obliged to God and to the monarch, who is obliged both to God and her people – seeking God's "honour and glory" and "study[ing] to preserve" the people "committed to her charge in welth, peace, and godlynes". The same injunctions carried over into what became King James's Book.

As a married man and father Shakespeare knew well the mutual obligations of wives and husbands, parents and children, as set out in the Bible, the Prayer Book and every text about social order, such as *The Boke of the Governor* (1531) by Sir Thomas Elyot, T.S. Eliot's ancestor; and in quitting Stratford for London he knew he was reneging on his husbandly and fatherly part. As an actor and shareholder in theatre companies he was locked into the mutual obligations of master-servant relations: the Lord Chamberlain's "Men" (1593-1599) were his "Servants"; their successor company, the King's "Men" of the Globe Theatre, were the King's "Servants". Title pages insisted so. The 1607 *Lear* is entered in the Stationers' Register 26 November 1607 as "A booke called Mr William Shakespeare his history of Kinge Lear as yt was played before the Kinges maiestie at Whitehall vppon St Stephans night at Christmas Last by his maiesties servantes playinge vsually at the globe on Banksyde..."

What the play recognises is what Shakespeare well knew, namely that not living up to your obligations could come more easily than doing your duty. Duty and dutifulness were not always pleasant. The etymology of *obligation* announced that: it's connected with *ligature* – convenient tyings, but also bondage, irksome bindings. *Obligation* is still commonly linked with forceful binding: *binding obligations*, we still say; *duty bound*; *what a bind* – language reflecting the irksomeness, the pain, of being tied. A play titled *King Lear* hints from the start that binding obligations, the bind of obligations, are going to be strongly in question, for this medieval king is named for a *lear*, in medieval English the term for the tape which is used to bind the otherwise loose edges of fabric. And *Lear*, reflecting extendedly on obligation, is a tragedy of disobliging.

Everything bad in the play follows from failures to meet what's obliged by personal and social status– massive renegings on personal, moral, social, political duty. The fundamental disruption is Lear's abdication, his attempt at laying aside the obligations of an anointed king to rule, swiftly finessed by reneging on fatherly obligations to daughter Cordelia and on lord and master obligations to his courtier-servant Kent, and then doing a Cordelia job on Cordelia's sisters. Fathers should not cast off children or loyal servants. Children are to be blessed not cursed.

For his part, Gloucester has cheerfully betrayed his wife and his marriage contract. He's too easily

Opposite: Galina Volchek as Regan in Grigori Kozintsev's 1970 film Korol Lir. *The film boasted an original score by Shostakovich, and used a 1949 translation by Boris Pasternak, author of* Dr Zhivago.

persuaded to turn on his son Edgar. Edmund plots against his half-brother, busting through any thought of brotherly obligation, turning father against son (and in the name of his very unnatural idea of what's natural), and not long afterwards assisting in the blinding of his own father. Goneril and Regan compete to betray their husbands sexually with Edmund. The blinding of Gloucester in his own home terrifyingly betrays the natural obligations of guests to hosts. "You are my guests;/ Do me no foul play, friends," he says, and

> *I am your host;*
> *With robbers' hands my hospitable favours*
> *You should not ruffle thus. (III.vii)*

Whatever goodness there is in this play arises along the axes of obligation. Cordelia and Edgar behave as dutiful children to their woefully aberrant fathers; Kent remains the staunchest of servants despite maltreatment at his master's whim; and the old men's reformations, such as they are, consist in being awakened to good, or at least better, fatherliness, and in Lear's case, a wising-up to some of the responsibilities of a monarch that he had hitherto ignored.

"O, I have ta'en/Too little care of this," he realises out in the storm, feeling now, we're supposed to believe, "what wretches feel" – though rather weakening the force of his new awakening by attacking others, piously urging "pomp" to take the medicine (the "physic") he's taking, feel what he's feeling, and shed their "superflux" to the poor, which is a bit rich coming from someone who's no longer in a position to be practically charitable. And, of course, a major horror of *Lear* is that the worst disobligers are well up on the obligation codes they flout. Gloucester's dismay at the breakdown of guest-host relations follows his earlier lament at "the bond cracked 'twixt father and son"(I.ii). Lear reminds Regan of "The offices of nature, bond of childhood/Effects of courtesy, dues of gratitude", wrongly thinking she'll pay the dues her sister hasn't. It's "filial ingratitude" which dements him.

Edmund is well aware that the breaks in

THE VILENESS OF REGAN

"As the play progresses, [Goneril and Regan] earn the joint title 'unnatural hags', but we come to recognize Goneril's superior intelligence and managerial skill and to see that Regan trails behind her, compensating for dullness with exaggerated brutality."
Stephen Booth

"Regan... has no ideas of her own, her special vileness is always to increase the measure of pain others are prepared to inflict; her mind is itself a lynch mob."
Stanley Cavell ■

child-parent relations that he's smearing
Edgar with and fomenting in Gloucester are
"unnaturalness". They're *dissolutions, diffidences,
dissipations* of family bonds. Goneril and Regan
are rather shocked at Lear's disowning of Cordelia
and banishment of Kent, temporarily awed at
the sort of disobligings (from "poor judgement",
"waywardness", "unconstant starts" (I.i)), which
they'll soon be monstrously multiplying themselves.

It is also mightily perturbing that the main
upholders of the obligation code can be thought of

"I AM YOUR HOST"

The handy-dandyish bond
between obligation and
disobligation is especially
animated in the use of the
word "host" (III.vii),
especially when used by
Gloucester. The French
philosopher and
deconstructionist Jacques
Derrida has dwelt at length
on its range of possible
meanings. Host can signify
a giver of hospitality, a
welcomer of guests, but also
a guest, the receiver of
hospitality; a host can be a
friend, but also an enemy, an
opponent, even an army of
hostiles; host is also the
word for a tortured victim
(as Christ on the cross,
represented in the Holy
Communion ceremony by
the wafer known as the
host). Derrida coins
hostipitality to catch these
contradictions (in his *Of
Hostipitality*, trans Rachel
Bowlby, 2000).
Hostipitality is rife in
Gloucester's career. "I am
your host"; but what is that?
A bestower of hospitality, a
receiver of it, a friend, an
opponent, a tortured victim?
He's variously all five ∎

as relaxing their grip: Edgar's withholding his identity from his father as long as he does smacks a bit of gratuitous filial cruelty; it's a protracted silence which disturbingly echoes the earlier, devastating refusal of Cordelia in the opening scene to give her doting daddy the flattery he craves. She talks of her "duties" and loving him "according to my bond", but there's room for thinking she was actually failing her "bond" as daughter in not doing the daughterly rhetorical business her sisters are so clever at. She rightly says her husband will have "Half my love", but at the moment she has no husband, and so no wifely obligations, only daughterly ones. Was France unceremoniously dumped from the play – going back home on the feeble grounds that he's just remembered some important unfinished business – so that Cordelia could give her father all her daughterly self?*

Plainly, the play's take on obligation is not simple. Kent's rival as loyalest servant is the egregious Oswald, Goneril's faithful attendant in wicked behaviour. And sometimes doing the moral thing means transgressing the code, as when Cornwall's "servant" in III.vii resists Cornwall's

*A thought Stephen Booth rather spoils by plausibly suggesting, in his extremely fruitful "Speculations on Doubling in Shakespeare Plays" – Appendix 2 of the always impressive *King Lear, Macbeth, Indefinition and Tragedy* (1983) – that France might have been written out because the actor playing him in scene one "may have played Edgar thereafter".

blinding of Gloucester with words about serving a higher, more moral cause: "I have served you ever since I was a child, /But..." Cornwall is horrified his "villain", a feudal tenant, should take up arms against his Lord. "A peasant stand up thus?" snaps Regan, killing him with a borrowed sword. It's a peasant revolt that is totally out of normal order but is admirable here and justified in extreme circumstances.

It is not unlike Albany turning against Goneril. Monstrous, tiger-like, *filth*, a *fiend* and morally *deformed*, she's forfeited any right to husbandly loyalty. In fact he'd kill her, except "A woman's shape doth shield thee"; he draws the line at the point where tradition says men are obliged not to hurt women physically. And the final words of the play's last scene are pretty wobbly about obligation. Faithful Kent talks principled obedience:

> *I have a journey, sir, shortly to go;*
> *My master calls me, I must not say no. (V.iii)*

But we never learn which master he's referring to, nor what he's demanding – suicide, some people think, which would be an invitation even the loyalest "servant" should resist. As for Edgar, he's torn between counter-obligations:

> *The weight of this sad time we must obey,*

John Gielgud as Lear and Peggy Ashcroft as Cordelia. John Gielgud first appeared as Lear in 1931. He directed himself in this 1950 production, and subsequently played Lear in a radio production at the age of 90.

Speak what we feel, not what we ought to say.
                                    (V.iii)

This echoes Albany, giving way to the obligation
to speak what he felt about his wife, rather than
keeping up orthodox husbandly speak.* And thus
we might think that the play's ending rather
sustains the hovering suggestion that obligation
and disobligation are a necessarily connected pair,
feeding parasitically off each other, all part of the
play's uncommitted, deconstructive handy-
dandyism (see pp.27-8; 36).

How important are the gods?

It's normal in *King Lear* for people to hold
transcendent powers – God, the gods, the heavens,
Nature, Fortune, the stars – responsible for driving
and controlling events, behaviour, character.
"Fortune... turn thy wheel," says Kent, in the stocks
(II.ii). Gloucester puts all recent bad things –
civil disorders, treasons, broken families – down
to planetary influence: "These late eclipses in
the sun and moon" (I.ii). Only astrological force
("the stars") can explain the character differences
between Cordelia and her sisters, thinks Kent

*In Q it is Albany who has this last word about differing
obligations.

(IV.iii). Albany thinks the deaths of Goneril and Regan a "judgement of the heavens" (V.iii), and that Cornwall's death-wound from the servant is the vengeance of the "Justicers" "above" (IV.ii). According to Gloucester the wishes of the gods for humans are "opposeless" (IV.vi), i.e. irresistible. (The word "opposeless" is a notable Shakespeare coinage.)

In fact the gods are treated as a kind of people's flexi-friend, up for whatever you wish by way of divine assistance. Edmund wants them to "stand up" for bastards (I.ii). Gloucester prays they'll bless Edgar (IV.vi), Cordelia that they'll "cure"

THE FOOL

Fools were court jesters and grand-household wits – men hired by kings, princes and other grandees to provoke, comment, stimulate, amuse. Lear's Fool pops in (I.iv) to a warmish welcome from his employer – "'How now, my pretty knave, how dost thou?" – and disappears as abruptly at III.vi, capping Lear's words from deep inside an upside-down mind – "We'll go to supper i' the morning" – with a sort of sarcastic echo: "And I'll go to bed at noon" (though only in F).*

There is only one mention of a fool after that.

*Oddly, "Go to bed at noon" is a folk-name of salsify, a flower which closes its petals at noon-time, and so has provoked some critical excitement, though the Fool's words might just be a way of saying "I'm off now".

Lear's mental derangements (IV.vii), Kent that they'll "shelter" banished Cordelia (I.i) and reward Gloucester's kindness towards mad Lear (II.vi). Lear invokes "the stored vengeance of heaven" to fall on Goneril's "ingrateful head" (II.ii). The "great gods" who are drenching him with the "dreadful pudder" (violent disturbance) of the storm should "Find out their enemies", the powerful immoral hypocrites who dish out the law (III.ii).

But for all this pretty universal faith in the interest of super-human powers there's also a lot of scepticism about, suggesting the gods and stars and so forth are actually disinterested, and that

---

"And my poor fool is hanged", says the dying Lear (V.iii). But he's lamenting the dead Cordelia. This has encouraged a traditional suggestion that the same actor played both Cordelia and the Fool, though this is not very likely, given that Shakespeare's Fool was, apparently, played by a middle-aged comic actor, Robert Armin, an ugly dwarfish man, whereas one would expect Cordelia to have been played by some prettier, fresher boy.

Armin was renowned as a vocalist, and probably sang the Fool's rhyming lines. No fool (Fools weren't), he published a much-reprinted satirical account of the Fool's social life and role, *Foole Upon Foole* (1600), in which he distinguished "natural" fools – men funny as such, comics who made you laugh by their very presence – from "artificial" fools, satirically smart with what Dickens, in *Hard Times*, calls "Shakespearian quips and retorts". Lear's Fool is an "artificial".

Dressed in Fool's "motley" (Q I.iv), the rough garment of a servant or idiot,

human actions are rather in human hands. "If it be you that stirs these daughters' hearts /Against their father," says Lear to "you gods" (II.ii). *If*. Edmund forcefully rebuts his father's astrological faith as "the excellent foppery of the world":

> *as if we were villains on necessity, fools by heavenly compulsion, knaves, thieves and treachers by spherical predominance; drunkards, liars and adulterers by an enforced obedience of planetary influence; and all that we are evil in by a divine thrusting on. An admirable evasion of whoremaster man, to lay his goatish disposition*

and a silly feathered hat, his "coxcomb" (I.iv), he looked stupid, even childish, waving a toy stick of some sort. His childishness is emphasized by Lear calling him "boy" and his calling Lear "nuncle" (that initial *n* drifted across from "an uncle" in the linguistic process known as metathesis).

But grown-up wisdoms pour from him, and he is cannily and annoyingly truthful about Lear's foolishness in giving up his kingdom, becoming a nothing – "an O without a figure", lacking a preceding number to make it something (I.iv) – treating Cordelia badly, putting faith in Regan (I.v), and so on.

In the mock-trial of Goneril he sits naturally on the judges' bench (II.vi). His wise jeers hurt; he suggests Lear's brains are in his heels now, so his gibes will give Lear kibes, chilblains, of the brain (I.v). No wonder Lear finds the Fool "bitter"(I.iv) and a "pestilent gall" (I.iv). He speaks, as the old adage puts it, truth to power. Zany and childish-looking, but full of adult wisdoms, the Fool is the walking

*on the charge of a star.... Fut! I should have been
that I am had the maidenliest star in the
firmament twinkled on my bastardizing. (I.ii)*

And he goes on to tease Edgar with Gloucester-
like suggestions about what the recent eclipses
portend – Edgar another sceptic who's amazed his
brother should have joined the "astronomical" sect
(I.ii). *Fut* is a very strong blasphemous oath, "By
Christ's Foot" (very close to the expletive *Fuck*).*

*It's only in Q: possibly cleaned out of the play after the May 1606
"Act to Restrain Abuses of Players", which banned "jesting" or
"profane" namings of God, Jesus Christ, the Holy Ghost or the
Trinity in dramatic performances.

embodiment of handy-
dandy. In I.iv he wants to
assign his fool's hat of office
– his coxcomb – to Lear the
real fool. On the heath this
"boy" plays the adult carer
("Good nuncle" in II.ii).

Tom of Bedlam's arrival
as a canny madman in Act
III to a great extent
duplicates the Fool's role,
and before long he drops
out. Can it be that
Shakespeare came to feel
that having mad Lear, mad
Tom and the Fool all
together on stage was
over-doing the craziness a
bit? In Adrian Noble's 1982

Royal Shakespeare
Company production the
Fool (Antony Sher) was
actually stabbed to death
by an angry Lear (Michael
Gambon).

At the end of III.ii (but
in F only) comes the Fool's
big set-piece moment,
prophesying as Merlin,
legendary Arthurian mage,
looking forward to the
future. And riddling and
incoherent the prophecy is.
First an anti-utopia is
envisaged, when current
bad behaviour by priests,
brewers, nobles and
heretic-burners carries on

Feelings about human responsibility plainly run high in the play. What's clearly at issue is just about the hottest Protestant theological potato of the day – whether the Calvinists or the Lutherans were right about free will. Martin Luther's followers thought you were free to choose to be saved from sin and hell, Jean Calvin's that you were "predestined" by God to salvation or damnation. You had no choice because God had "foreordained" your choices.

But, characteristically, the play refuses to take sides, just as it never arbitrates in the running disagreement over the nature of the divine. Are the

(which is presumably what nobody would wish); second, a real utopia, when there'll be justice in law, slander ceases, cutpurses stop working thronged places like theatres, moneylenders function openly, and pimps and whores build churches (all pretty desirable). All this will amount to a "great confusion" for the country, Albion – though surely only the first, anti-utopia would be confusing – and be a time when "going shall be used with feet" (no change there then).

It is weird stuff, indeed, confused about "confusion", about what prophecies are customarily about, and mixing the line between desirable and undesirable futures – fitting, though, for a master of handy-dandy. It's impossible to clear up the mystery, though editors have tried – bluffing in their footnotes and desperately shuffling the futurist items around. Nahum Tate ducked the problem by dropping the Fool altogether. Some modern productions follow suit; others, embarrassed by this particular enigmatic stuff, ditch the passage ∎

gods *just* (Edgar, V.iii), *gentle* (Gloucester, IV.vi), *kind* (Cordelia, IV.vii), bountiful with blessings ("The bounty and the benison": Gloucester, IV.vi)? Or are they coldly neglectful (France, I.i), and positive only in dishing out horrible vengeance on transgressive humans? That's Albany's view: the "judgement of the heavens" in having Goneril and Regan killed "makes us tremble", but he takes it as par for the course (V.iii) – a sadist's idea of divine justice. Edgar thinks it just that the gods turn "our pleasant vices" round on us, and so sex with Edmund's mother has cost Gloucester his eyes (V.iii). On his agonised road to Dover (IV.i) Gloucester chimes in: the gods are like *Clockwork Orange* yobs, picking on people to squash them like flies:

> *As flies to wanton boys are we to the gods,*
> *They kill us for their sport.*

But who's right about God? The play refuses handydandyishly to come down on any side.

So how Christian is *Lear*?

So much God-talk, but what do we make of the play's Christian themes and suggestions? Their degree and nature sharply divide critics, with

Opposite: Romola Garai as Cordelia in the 2007 RSC production

believers and Christian sympathisers toughing it out with sceptics and atheists along tightly drawn ideological battle-lines.

Shakespeare did, of course, have to be careful in addressing Christian matters: that 1606 Act stood in the way of directly talking about the Christian God on stage. But everybody in Shakespeare's highly churched audience would have heard and recognised the play's Christian and Biblical noises (Protestant Geneva Bible noise), and known what all the prayers and god-talk were about. Everyone would have spotted straightaway that all the talk of gods, heavens, stars, and so forth was code for the Christian God – unlike so many modern literary critics who seem to think the play's religiosity is pagan or otherwise pre-Christian, and the like-minded directors who fill their stages with Druids, men in cave-man rig and the like. It's hard to imagine a contemporary who would not have seen Kent and Lear's swearing by Greek Apollo and Roman Jupiter and his wife Juno as rather unsubtle subterfuge (I.i; II.ii), and actually relished the play's theological stirrings as touching matters of intense current interest – about, for instance, grace.

Grace – goodwill; favouring, benignant regard – was a very contentious contemporary theological issue. All churches and sects saw God as the gracious donor of the gift of forgiveness and salvation to sinful humanity, the gift embodied in God's Son Jesus, who gives up heaven and divinity to effect redemption by his death. The gift which should be accepted by humankind in gratitude – with a good grace, as it were. What was contentious was the detail. The Lutheran Reformation was based in an insistence on the utterly gratuitous nature of grace. It was a totally free gift, freely offered, generously and "generally" distributed to all humans who all had a free will to receive it. Unlike medieval Roman Catholicism, which made you earn the gift, with good works, penances and so forth. And different, too, from the Calvinist strictures which made God gratuitous in the modern sense of arbitrary and picky in his giving, bestowing grace only on a selected few, the "elected", "predestined" ones. They had no free will in the matter. In the elaborated Calvinist doctrine, Christ's atonement was "limited", and God's gift of grace "irresistible". The offer of salvation was "particular", not "general".

Like the Christian deity, kings were thought of as having the good gift of grace to bestow. Lear has grace, indeed he is grace, is graciousness in person. "[H]ere's grace," says the Fool pointing to Lear (III.ii). Lear banishes Cordelia "Without our grace" (I.i). She regrets she no longer "stands within his grace" (I.i). In putting Kent in the stocks, Cornwall offends the king's "grace" (II.ii). And at the root of the play's distresses is the terrible blend in Lear of the old Roman Catholic divinity whose grace is not free, and the Calvinist one who is arbitrary in his giving. Lear wants to manifest his grace in a would-be God-like bestowal of power and possessions on his daughters. In fact he proposes giving up everything, in imitation of Jesus, agent and essence of God's free gift of grace. "The subject of *Lear* is renunciation," George Orwell cannily suggested, but missing the spilt theology of *Lear*'s transactions. A. D. Nuttall, in *Shakespeare the Thinker*, is the only *Lear* critic I know to pick up on the sub-theological awkwardness involved.

Lear's intended largesse is focused on Cordelia. She's been selected for the best portion. She's to be the "particular" blessed one, as opposed to her sisters who are more "general" recipients. But none of his gifting comes free; like a pastiche medieval deity he wants payment – a dole-out of flattery. Like pre-Reformation Christians Goneril and Regan are quick to pay up, to make an exchange of gifts. Like a good Protestant, Cordelia will have none of such transacting – which makes her "ingrateful" (II.ii); as, very soon, all mankind is (III.ii). For Goneril and Regan quickly dock their giving, neglecting to go on paying their "dues of gratitude" (II.ii).

What's morally impressive about Cordelia's career is that she's so forgiving of her dis-graceful father, making up for her sisters' lacks of gratitude, giving goodwill in exchange for her father's earlier lack of it. It is no wonder that, returned from

France, she's haloed in Christian rhetoric, perceived as a heavenly person, an angel, a Christ-like saviour bringing redemption into a fallen world and particularly to the father who viciously disowned her. Like Jesus, she's grace in person. A Gentleman tells Kent that Cordelia's tears upon reading of her father's plight in the stormy night were "holy water" shaken "from her heavenly eyes" (Q IV.iii). She's the daughter as Christ-like child, at least when she apostrophises Lear in a kind of prayer: "O dear father, /It is thy business that I go about" (IV.iv) – quoting the boy Jesus in the Gospels, telling his parents he "must go about my Father's [i.e. God's] business" (Luke 2.49). United with her, the physically broken and mentally shattered Lear thinks he's a dead sinner "bound/ Upon a wheel of fire" in hell, meeting "a soul in bliss", a "spirit" from heaven (IV.vii).

Later, captured by Edmund's thugs and facing imprisonment, Lear tells her that, in the cage, he'll kneel down and ask her "forgiveness" (when she's inclined to "ask me blessing"), and that they'll "live/ And pray" together, and "take upon's the mystery of things/As if we were God's spies" – pious anticipations capped by his declaring that "Upon such sacrifices, my Cordelia,/The gods themselves throw incense", as they're hauled off to prison (V. iii). He seems to be hinting that Cordelia's life and death are as sacrificial as Christ's – Christian priests traditionally cast incense on the

Eucharistic altar or Holy Communion table. The hint fits those earlier words from another Gentleman as the crazed Lear scampered away from his rescuers:

> *Thou hast one daughter*
> *Who redeems nature from the general curse*
> *Which twain have brought her to. (IV.vi)*

In the Bible's Grand Narrative of salvation Jesus's "sacrificial" death on the cross redeemed humanity (nature) from the "general curse" brought about by the transgression of the "twain", or pair, of original sinners Adam and Eve. This Gentleman sees Cordelia as playing Christ in the play's fallen world of rampant evil brought about by a wicked pair of Adam-and-Eve-like sisters.

Lear carrying in the dead Cordelia at the end has reminded many viewers of that traditional Christian iconography, the Pietà, a painting or sculpture of Mary the Mother of Jesus holding her dead son on her lap or in her arms. The Christian critic Stephen Medcalf is rightly compelled, as others have been, by the religious atmosphere of this moment, and the play's associated Biblical rhetoric. These include, for Medcalf, hearing the Beatitude – "Blessed are the merciful, for they shall obtain mercy" (Matthew 5.7) – in Lear's talk about kneeling and asking forgiveness when Cordelia asks for a blessing. And

A.D. Nuttall is at his most moving in *Shakespeare the Thinker* when he confesses to having his own non-Christian reading "shaken" by Medcalf's essay.*

But the religious imagery associated with Cordelia is not enough to shake any of the downright unbelievers. George Orwell is quite blunt in his "Lear, Tolstoy and the Fool" essay: the "morality of Shakespeare's later tragedies is not religious in the ordinary sense, and certainly is not Christian". For his part, lifelong Christian-God hater William Empson, in the canny "Fool in Lear" chapter of his wonderful *The Structure of Complex Words* (1951; 1985), is happy to see the divinities of *Lear* as "malicious" and "criminal lunatics", and prayers to them as the perennial agent of un-good. "Every time Lear prays to the gods, or anyone else prays on his behalf, there are bad effects immediately."

The play's late talk of forgiveness by Lear is,

*Nuttall doesn't let on that Medcalf's essay, "Dreaming, Looking, and Seeing: Shakespeare and a Myth of Resurrection", started life in a 2004 symposium in Nuttall's honour, or that his (Nuttall's) own "Last Word" in the published conference proceedings, *Thinking with Shakespeare: Comparative and Interdisciplinary Essays for A.D. Nuttall* (2007), is considerably less shaken by Medcalf's long-held persuasions. Like a Shakespearian gentleman, Nuttall forebears on either occasion from alluding to his old friend's dafter tunings in of Christian notes, such as his thinking that Lear's description of Cordelia's death by hanging as one of life's ravaging "crosses" affirms her dying as a parallel of Christ's crucifixion.

for Empson, contaminated by his "imbecility". The final reunion of Lear and Cordelia – characterised by such "divine goodness and gentleness" – "stands out in memory", and may even appear to change "the 'meaning' of the play, which would then be one of regeneration". But this gentling of Lear does not hold water: "this mood of greatness arises in him [Lear] as a sort of wild flower, almost unconnected with anything else". If this is theology, it's terribly "limited".

And Empson's strong scepticism is more than endorsed by Jonathan Dollimore in his influential slash-and-burn neo-Marxist "materialist" critique, *Radical Tragedy: Religion, Ideology and Power in the Drama of Shakespeare and His Contemporaries* (1984). Lear's suffering and Cordelia's death are

LEAR AND HOLY COMMUNION

The scepticism about language in the play registered in its persistent crisis of deixis or reference (see pp.85-6) is, of course, overhung by the great contemporary argy-bargy between Protestants and Catholics over the nature of the eucharistic bread and wine. "This is my body," said Jesus at the Last Supper, pointing at the bread and wine; "hoc est enim meum corpus" in the words of the Latin mass.

But the Christian world was completely divided over what precisely Jesus and the repeated eucharistic words were pointing to. What sort

no Christianised story, nor even the post-Christian "humanist" one popular with some critics, in which people learn wisdom and authentication of being of a non-transcendent kind – an existentialism Dollimore finds to be merely parodic of the Christian story which he says is utterly non-existent in the play.

Dollimore's line is that the sufferings of Lear and Gloucester are not in aid of some moral, soul-saving induction into new compassion but of the more important radical raising of materialist awareness of bad social conditions and power relations – though why there can't be both of these effects is never explained. "To see [Cordelia's] death as intrinsically redemptive is simply to mystify both her and her death." The pity and

---

of "body" was indicated by hoc est/this is? It was one of the absolute sticking points in the Reformation and after. More blood had been spilt over those two words, *hoc est*, than over any other pair in history, observed Michel Montaigne, Shakespeare's favourite French philosopher. Roman Catholics thought the bread and wine were "transubstantiated" literally into Christ's body and blood; Lutherans thought the bread and wine metaphorically Christ's body; Calvin suggested they were metonyms of that body.

The pervasive crisis of deixis, the deictic paralysis, in *Lear* hints at Shakespeare's tactical neutrality over yet one more bone of contention dividing Rome and the Reformed Church of England; it's a marker of Shakespeare's persistent refusal to come clean in the contemporary wars of religion ∎

kindness that Lear learns, and she stands for, are ineffectual and, far from being redemptive, are ideologically complicit with the "power structure" which is in practice destroying them.

Dollimore lines up a huge cast of voices more or less contemporary with Shakespeare's in aid of his scathing anti-Christian – and anti-humanist – take on selfhood, ethics and politics in *Lear* and its time. Thomas More, Castiglione, Machiavelli, Montaigne, Hobbes are all paraded, though not very convincingly. As Tom McAlindon relishingly shows in *Shakespeare Minus "Theory"* (2004), Dollimore reads all these writers with slanting prejudice. And some of Dollimore's local "materialist" readings of the play are just plain wrong – as when he misunderstands Lear's disclaiming of all "property of blood" (I.i), as revealing Lear's paternalistic belief that fathers commodify daughters as pieces of owned property, whereas *property* in this context means the intrinsic character of a blood-relation; or when he weirdly mistakes the Gentleman's metaphor of Cordelia's tears of distress dropping from her eyes like "pearls from diamonds" (IV.iii), as showing that he thinks her emotion is "a kind of passive female commodity".

It would be wrong, though, to dismiss the scepticisms of Dollimore, Orwell and Empson, and the wariness of many other modern readers, as merely the resistance of paid-up anti-Christian, anti-transcendentalist ideologues. To be sure, *Lear* is ghosted by echoes from the Christian narrative of God's grace and salvation, in which fallen sinful nature is redeemed by the sacrificial sufferings of Christ, but these are mainly tantalising hints. There's something up with much, if not all, of the Christian, Biblical referencing. It's commonly ironic stuff. Cordelia, for instance, going about her father's business repeats Jesus's words rejecting his human parents' wishes for him; they're the words of a disobedient child.

The so-called Pietà of the finale is a warped, even parodic one – the agony of a father, not of a mother – advertising the curious absence of Cordelia's mother from the story. Miracles don't happen. In that haunting muddled talk by Kent in the stocks (II.ii) – inviting "heaven's benediction" to illuminate Cordelia's letter about her seeking "remedies" for losses – "miracles" are said to be what "Nothing almost sees", i.e. what the poor "almost" see. *Almost*. And neither they, nor we, do see any.

And Cordelia dies – the pointless end of "persecuted virtue", as the eminently Christian Dr Johnson put it. He preferred the good Christian Nahum Tate's version of *King Lear* in which Cordelia "retired with victory and felicity". Shakespeare's version flouted Johnson's sense of a divinely ordered just world – no hint of Christian resurrection, of a cheerful afterlife for the righteous.

She's "dead as earth", Lear grieves; no Christian hopes there. For all its many Christian hints and guesses, the play resolutely refuses to close on them. But that they are there does mean, for all Dollimore's certainties, that there's no absolutely anti-Christian closure either.

What are we supposed to make of Bedlam Tom's gibberish?

The play's position on Christianity is simply hard to read. It would help us if we knew for certain whether Shakespeare was a Roman Catholic (his family was), or, more likely, whether he was, as Stephen Greenblatt paints him in *Hamlet in Purgatory* (2001), torn conflictedly between the rival theologies and practices of the Catholicism he was brought up in and the revived Protestantism imposed by the Elizabethan state.

But the play's various Roman Catholic and Protestant thrusts point unhelpfully in different directions. There's certainly a failure to take sides in the play's visitings of the Roman Catholic-Protestant Calvin-Luther free-grace, free-will debates. Lear's Calvinist-type arbitrariness goes awfully wrong, but then so also does his pastiche Roman Catholic belief that godlike benefits are for sale. Lear's final scene with Cordelia does indeed enact a kind of "Pietà", but one so distorted it might almost amount to a dig at Roman Catholic Mariolatry, the cult of the Virgin Mary.

And what Mad Tom's babbling is meant to suggest is truly confusing. Edgar/Tom's words draw heavily on the anti-Jesuit pamphlet by the crusading anti-Catholic (and anti-Calvinist) preacher, Samuel Harsnett; but what is Shakespeare getting at by incorporating Harsnett's words? Does giving Harsnett's words to a lunatic indicate scepticism about Calvinism? Or does the blatant pretence of Tom's demon-possession

SAMUEL HARSNETT

It's long been known that *Lear* is full of things lifted from Samuel Harsnett's *A Declaration of Egregious Popish Impostures*, an official Privy Council publication (1603), and a jeering lampoon of Jesuit exorcism-practices, suggesting they are no more than faked-up religious theatre. The Revd Samuel Harsnett was a senior Cambridge academic and churchman (later an MP and Archbishop of York), a very hot Protestant and a very well-known anti-Calvinist.

The American critic Stephen Greenblatt gave Harsnett prominence in his New Historical readings of theatricality and the devil in *Lear* – see his

mean Shakespeare is lining up with Harsnett's view that the Jesuits' faith in demon-possession is faked-up nonsense and Roman Catholic nonsense to boot? But what if we're to suppose Tom's fakery is all in a good cause – enabling him to get helpfully alongside mad Lear – and thus a kind of model of the good that theatre (basically all pretence and fiction) can achieve?

It's hard to tell. Intriguingly the same religious double bill of Calvinism and Jesuits crops up in *Lear*'s great 1606 contemporary *Macbeth*, where predestination seems to get satirised in terms of Macbeth's being determined by the Witches' predictions, and Jesuit untruthfulness

Shakespearean Negotiations (1988). But long before this, Kenneth Muir listed the many references to Harsnett's book in a *Review of English Studies* article of 1951 (all in Appendix 7 of Muir's excellent 1952 Arden *Lear*).

Much prominent stuff in the play came from Harsnett, including the name Edmund (chief of Harsnett's crooked priests was a Father Edmunds); and those *corky* arms of Gloucester which Cornwall orders bound for the blinding (III.vii); and Lear's curious *hysterica passio* (II. ii), literally a sickness of the womb, a traditional problem of pregnant women – the "mother" as Lear calls it – which the brother of one of Harsnett's Jesuits was said to suffer from; and, extendedly, Tom's crazed chatter about demons called Obidicut, Hobbidance, Mahu, Modo, Flibbertigibbet, *mopping* and *mowing* and *possessing* women. (III.iv; IV.i) ▪

comes in the play's gibing in the Porter scene at the word *equivocator*?*

But how do we understand the Christmas 1609 performance of *Lear* at Gowthwaite Hall in Yorkshire for a recusant audience of northern Roman Catholics? Did they, mindful of the persecution and execution of Roman Catholics, take the play as being about "the sufferings of the righteous in pagan times", as Stephen Medcalf suggests? Or did they think, like Richard Wilson (in *Secret Shakespeare: studies in theatre, religion and resistance*, 2004), that the role played by not speaking-out in *Lear* sympathetically registered the plight of English Roman Catholics compelled to silence and closetedness in a Protestant police-state? Did they perhaps think Harsnett was being satirised, in that its so-called fakeries are promulgated by a madman? That we'll never know is symptomatic, for the play sits as handydandyishly on the fence in these religious matters as in all its serious engagements.

Equivocation became famous during the trial in March 1606 of Jesuit Father Henry Garnet. At his trial for his part in the Catholic Gunpowder Plot of November 5th 1605, he attempted to justify his "equivocation", not telling the whole truth, because it was in a righteous cause (standard medieval moral-theology). He was put to death in May 1606 in the usual way of disembowelling and hanging.

Why is Edgar so important?

What Edgar/Tom does and says, however, seems to matter. He feels important, not least because of his massive verbal contribution. Only Lear himself has more lines. He's more important even than Cordelia, Harold Bloom thinks (in *Shakespeare the Invention of the Human*). In his verbal abundance he certainly does keep sounding like a focaliser, a main focal point of the play's personal, ethical, religious and political concerns. What we make of him and what he says is going greatly to influence what we think the play is about.

He is an Elizabethan/Jacobean Christian – at least he's been "christened", that is baptised as an infant, for he is, as Regan reveals, Lear's "godson", (II.i.) (Godfather Lear: now there's a thought...) He's the play's obviously good son, the innocent victim of his treacherous half-brother Edmund, repaying his father's hostility with loving-kindness – male double of Cordelia. He feels and enacts the socially and morally encoded obligations of a son, which weigh heavily on him. In the last words of the play, which F assigns to him, his concern is all with obligations – what we, who *shall* "never see so much", *must* obediently do, and what we *ought not* to say: the weighty last words of the man who's

acted as a kind of moral reflector, a conduit for sympathy, outrage and critique.

He's been a parallel Fool in fact, with the difference that his critical sympathising with Lear and Gloucester has been practical, not just verbal. On the run, he puts himself in the abject position of a Bedlam beggar, becoming one with the poorest of the poor, down among the destitute living below a human level. He takes

> *the basest and most poorest shape*
> *That ever penury in contempt of man*
> *Brought near to beast. (II.ii)*

(Notice the wonderfully emphatic double superlative: *most poorest*.) It's a deliberate stripping, filthying up, reduction, that makes him the play's quintessential "poor, bare, forked animal", the inspiration for Lear's own stripping off (III.iv.105-7). Elizabethan and Jacobean audiences would recognise in Edgar's self-abasement echoes of the well-known theological story of Jesus's incarnation, the Son of God quitting the splendours of heaven for abased human existence, going about in disguise, the heavenly Saviour among his people, enduring their pains and suffering in order to redeem them from such awfulness.

Scapegoating – the Biblical idea of the redemptive suffering of an outcast individual, which attaches to Cordelia – attaches also to Edgar. His "heart breaks", he says, at the aweing sight of mad Lear and blind Gloucester together (IV.vi). A. C. Bradley thought Edgar "the most religious person in the play". He's certainly a practical moral agent: his killing of Oswald when Oswald is about to kill Gloucester comes with his *précis* of Oswald's nauseous character as ironically loyal servant in a bad cause:

> *a serviceable villain,*
> *As duteous to the vices of thy mistress*
> *As badness would desire. (IV.vi)*

The gods are certainly on Edgar's mind as demanding loyalty, alongside the more mundane demands of kindred and king, when he kills Edmund:

> *False to thy gods, thy brother and thy father,*
> *Conspirant 'gainst this high illustrious prince,*
> *And from th'extremest upward of thy head*
> *To the descent and dust below thy foot*
> *A most toad-spotted traitor. (V.iii)*

And when he urges *patience*, the uncomplaining endurance of suffering, on Gloucester ("Bear free and patient thoughts", IV.vi) he tunes into the Bible's Job, famous for his patience.

But Edgar's wisdoms about individual suffering ("Who alone suffers, suffers most i' the mind", II.vi

Q); about living as "The lowest and most dejected thing of fortune" (IV.i); and about enduring life calmly in the face of death –

> *Men must endure*
> *Their going hence even as their coming hither.*
> *Ripeness is all. (V.ii)*

– are more Stoical than Biblical. Simon Palfrey actually labels Edgar a "Stoic philosopher" (in the

LETTERS IN *LEAR*

Letters pass to and fro busily in this play: the one Edmund forges in Edgar's name; the correspondence of Goneril and Regan; Cordelia's letter Kent reads in the stocks; the "dangerous" letter about Cordelia and her comrades-in-arms, possession of which hastens Gloucester's blinding; the one from Goneril which prompts Regan to commission Oswald to kill Gloucester; Edmund's note to the prison which is Cordelia's death-sentence; Edgar's challenge letter which helps trap Edmund.

The play even connects the nearly absolute fearfulness of letters with what are suggested as some intrinsically dubious aspects of the very letters of the alphabet which letters, of course, consist of. When in II.ii Kent catches Oswald carrying Goneril's "letters against the King", he calls him a "whoreson zed', an "unnecessary letter". Kent would like to "tread this unbolted [lumpy, effeminate] villain into mortar and daub the wall of a jakes with him". The letter Z is "unnecessary" because its

sharp Edgar section of the always canny *Doing Shakespeare*, 2005). It's no accident that his "Ripeness is all" speech should look forward to the outright Stoicism of Samuel Beckett and Pozzo's angry take in *Waiting for Godot* on life as a brief endurance test:

One day we were born, one day we shall die...
They give birth astride of a grave, the light gleams
an instant, then it's night once more.

functions can mostly be performed by S, and it doesn't occur in Latin. Oswald, and Goneril's letter, are word-stuff that Kent and the cause of good could do without. They're like graffiti, filthy words scribbled on lavatory walls: which is why Kent would like to plaster the wall of a "jakes", a shit-house, with the postman carrying Goneril's morally filthy correspondence.

The awfulness of letters is based in their performative force; they're writings that get things done, and, strikingly in this play, usually for the worse. Nothing must come, Lear says, between his "power"' and his "sentences" (I.i). So many letters, like Lear's sentences, have terrible power because they're death-sentences – like the killing sentence inscribed by a writing-machine's penknife on the body of the condemned man in Kafka's terrible story "In the Penal Settlement".

The letters in *Lear* can be thought of as strong reflectors of their author's gloom, panic even, about his own craft of letters, his own wielding of sentences. They offer a pretty grim picture of how dangerous contemporary writing could be. In Shakespeare's time men frequently ended up in exile, in jail and on the executioner's block because of what they wrote ■

Royal Mail stamp to celebrate the 50th anniversary of the Royal Shakespeare Company issued in 2011, featuring Paul Schofield as Lear in the 1962 production. The critic Kenneth Tynan declared of his performance: "You will never see such another."

TEN FACTS
ABOUT *KING LEAR*

1.

The only recorded performance during Shakespeare's lifetime was on 26th December 1606 at court. The Stationers' Register of November 26 1607 reports that *King Lear* was "played before the King's Majesty at Whitehall upon S. Stephen's night at Christmas last". It is generally thought that Richard Burbage played King Lear, John Hemmings was Gloucester, and Robert Armin played the Fool.

2.

For 142 years, from 1681 to 1823, *King Lear* was performed only in Nahum Tate's version, in which Lear, Gloucester and Cordelia survive, Cordelia marries Edgar, and there is no fool. Nahum Tate's version was criticised by Joseph Addison, Charles Lamb and William Hazlitt, but Samuel Johnson defended the poetic justice of it. Charles McCready revived the original *King Lear* in 1838, playing Lear himself. He also reintroduced the fool, whose part Tate had cut because he felt it was too frivolous.

3.

Jean-Luc Godard and Menahem Golan, of Cannon Films, are said to have signed the contract for the 1987 film version of *King Lear* at the 1985 Cannes Film Festival on a napkin. Golan and Godard are reported to have had lunch together, and signed the contract on a handy napkin. Golan gave Godard $20, 000 on the spot.

4.

Ian McKellen played Lear in Trevor Nunn's 2007 production wearing two wedding rings: he'd had an "epiphany", he said, that Lear's daughters had two different mothers, both now dead, Cordelia's dying in childbirth. (A fanciful backstory to cover the startling absence of mothers from this family drama, it fits in with Kent's incredulity (IV.iii.35-6) that the self-same "mate and make", wife and husband, could produce such different offspring.)

5.

Everyone knows the storm scene is located on a "blasted heath" but "heath" is not Shakespeare's word; it comes from a stage direction in Nicholas Rowe's 1709 edition.

6.

It is important that the actor playing Lear shouldn't be too feeble to lift the dead Cordelia, nor Cordelia too hefty for her death scene. In the Ankara State Theatre production of 1981, for instance, two muscular Turkish soldiers had to carry in Cordelia behind the howling Cüneyt Gökçer, the theatre's aged director, set on playing Lear despite his physical frailty. Better that than dropping her – which has been known to happen.

7.

The youngest actor ever to play Lear in a professional production was Nonso Anozie, who was 23 when he took the title role in Declan Donnellan's production for the RSC in 2002. In contrast, when Alvin Epstein played Lear for the Boston Actors' Theater in 2006, he was at 81 probably the actor closest in age to Lear himself.

8.

In Rupert Goold's 2009 Young Vic production, quickly dubbed the "soap opera" version, Lear sang bits of "My Way" at the beginning and the Fool trilled "Singing in the Rain" during the Storm (while Lear in a floral dress bellowed through a microphone).

9.

During the long madness of King George III, 1788-1820, stage productions of *King Lear* were banned in England because Lear's madness was too reminiscent of George's. In Alan Bennett's play *The Madness of King George*, the mad King insists on a reading from Lear IV.vii, the reunion of Lear and Cordelia.

10.

Kent is given some ingenious insults to throw at Goneril's servant, Oswald - including 'Thou whoreson zed, thou unnecessary letter!' and one of only two references to football in Shakespeare: 'you base football player.' (The other footballing reference comes in *The Comedy of Errors*.)

And even if we can construe the Stoicism as being close to a Biblical kind of patience, the play's apparently Christianised goodness does come with some perturbing aspects. For instance, why does Edgar conceal his true identity from his father for as long as he does? This maintenance of a cruel silence is forbiddingly reminiscent of Cordelia's daughterly refusal which provoked so much trouble.

And the Dover Cliffs fraud feels like the cruel acme of an altogether unnecessarily protracted deceiving. It's *grotesquely* tragi-farcical, G. Wilson Knight thought, with righteous indignation, in his strong reading of "King Lear and the Comedy of the Grotesque" (in his justly much reprinted 1930 book *The Wheel of Fire: Interpretations of Shakespearian Tragedy*, with its approving Preface by T.S. Eliot): "The grotesque merged into the ridiculous reaches a consummation in this bathos of tragedy." And are the Harsnett words in Bedlam Tom's mouth indicative of some inbuilt slipperiness, even fraudulence, in religious pretension *as such*, not just among Harsnett's Jesuit targets? Isn't Edgar's slick manipulation of roles – so many personae, so many voices, such multivalent concealment on a grand scale ("Edgar I nothing am", II.ii) – as much indicative of a ready liar and deceiver, of personal and moral insincerity even emptiness, as it is of a commendable capacity for useful part-playing and role-switching?

He is, as Simon Palfrey nicely points out, a formidable shape-shifter, now a gibbering madman, now a reader of Harsnett, now a proto-Christian preacher, a returned son and brother, a yokel killer of Oswald, an avenging knight, an earl, an heir apparent, as well as, in the "Dover cliffs" episode, an idiot guide, a "better spoken" assistant, a poetic travel agent, a recipient of charitable alms, and a bold peasant. Such stagey versatility betokens, one might think, a rather unstable self, an instability prominent even in the play's large scene of puzzled selfhood – commanded by Lear's "Who am I?" (I.iv), and "Who is it that can tell me who I am?" (I.iv). And Edgar is, of course, at the heart of the play's linguistic collapse: "O do, de, do, de, do, de," he gibbers (III.iv), the muttering dodedodedodeman himself.

But, again, just how sincere is that dodedodeism? How far is it just some gibberish put on to bolster the Bedlam Tom act? And how seriously can we take Tom's advice to Lear about avoiding brothels, not going into debt, and so forth, coming as it does at the end of a long invented autobiographical sketch about his being a no-good courtier, who did "the act of darkness" with a lustful mistress, drinking, gambling and fornicating too much, treacherous and violent, altogether an animal ("hog in sloth, fox in stealth, wolf in greediness, dog in madness", III.iv)?

There's satire of courtiers going on here, plainly, but it does nonetheless implicate Edgar rather as what D. J. Enright thinks of as a prig: "Such a dreary and heartless moraliser, with a pronounced inclination to priggishness." He does indeed tend to what the generally wise Stanley Cavell, in "The Avoidance of Love" chapter of his *Disowning Knowledge; In Six Plays of Shakespeare*, agrees is self-righteousness – or worse, to a terrible, even psychotic, puritan body revulsion in which sex is always "the act of darkness".

HUMAN ANIMALS

❝The extraordinary proliferation of animal imagery and references to animals has often been noted. These references include – dog, cur, rats, monkeys, ant, eels, vulture, wolf, frog, toad, tadpole, newt, mice, foxes, cats, greyhound, worms, adders – this list is by no means exhaustive. The general feeling is that the human world is being rapidly taken over by animals – palaces seem to be repossessed by dogs and foxes and snakes and other low, mean, snapping and sliding animals. There is no sense of magnificent animal energy, rather of things that prowl and creep and slither – sharp-toothed yet devoid of valour and glamour. One of the horrors of the play is the sense of the fading away of the human while such animals scurry and leap and slip into the play from every side. But it is the humans who are reverting – degenerating – to animals. Goneril and Regan end up as 'adders!' squinting at each other. Edmund turns out to be a 'foul-spotted toad'.

There's not much that's more appalling in *Lear*, thinks Harold Bloom, than when Edgar, central apostle of love in Bloom's reading, lines up with Lear's deranged rant against the bestial hell – "darkness... sulphurous pit, burning, scalding, stench, consumption" (IV.vi) – of women's private parts, in talking casually to Edmund about the justice of the gods in allowing Gloucester's blinding as a punishment for sexual pleasures, in particular sex outside marriage with Edmund's mother.

The relapse, or regression, is, we feel, to some prior stage of evolution when things had but recently crawled out of the mud. These animals are not fine enough to be man's competitors; they are rather his mean ancestors. Yet how quickly they can repossess his world – how easily he can re-become them. So near is the ditch; so easy is the fall back into the slime. It is the copious listing of such encroaching and invading animals, or animalised humans, that gives such agonising force to Lear's final complaint against the universe:

Why should a dog, a horse,
a rat, have life
And thou no breath at all?
Thou'lt come no more,
Never, never, never, never,
never. (V.iii)

That line must be the most appalling in literature. This is a world in which rats retain all their mean, scurrying activity while Cordelia is hanged in lonely squalor by a paid murderer. And will come no more. This is unbearable. Who would want to see as well, or as much, as this? **"**

Tony Tanner, *Introduction to Shakespeare's Tragedies*, Vol 1, Everyman's Library, Dent, 1992-3 ∎

The gods are just and of our pleasant vices
Make instruments to plague us:
The dark and vicious place where thee he got
Cost him his eyes. (V.iii.168-171)

This is, as D. J. Enright points out, "barbaric" Old Testament morality: "scarcely Christian one would have thought". It's certainly not what Enright thinks of as religious:

> Bradley remarks that he [Edgar] is "the most religious person in the play". If this is true, it is extra evidence that the play is not religious in any sense of the word that springs to mind.

But, of course, the Old Testament religious vision of God rewarding the unrighteous with horrible affliction and pain was widely held in Shakespeare's time by Christians, especially those puritanical ones who shared Edgar's and Lear's professed stock of body horrors. *Precisians*, they were labelled, the religiously over-strict: perpetual target of Elizabethan and Jacobean drama, not least of Shakespeare. (Recall Angelo in *Measure for Measure*, and Malvolio in *Twelfth Night*.) And though it seems pretty clear what Shakespeare thought of them and their body revulsions, it's never absolutely clear how far Edgar's priggishness is being offered as simply moral and religious delusion. Which is, once more, symptomatic of the

play's refusal of certainty and closure, its not
licensing any spokesman whose word and actions

Ian McKellen as Lear in Trevor Nunn's 2007 production. Germaine Greer wrote of the production:
"The most memorable moment, for many of us the only memorable moment, in Trevor Nunn's latest
production of King Lear is when Ian McKellen drops his trousers and displays his impressive
genitalia to the audience."

might be thought to go as the play's meaning, not even Edgar the apparent focaliser, the man allowed the play's haunted last word (at least in F).

To what extent is Nature being questioned?

From the start it's not just religion that's at stake, but nature, what's felt to be natural, the accepted natural order. Cordelia's silence is conventionally unnatural. Lear's division-scheme assumes Cordelia's portion of territory goes with her as marriage portion. Her silence undercuts that ancient patriarchal equation between daughters and property. It's an upsetting of the assumed natural order, an offence against "nature" in the form of daughters' subordination to fathers. For nature, what's natural, was what was supposed to be inborn, what should characterise you as a member of a kindred, a kin, a kinship, your family. In Shakespeare's time *kind*, out of the Germanic verbal pot, meant *nature* – the equivalent word from the Latinate pot. Being kind, in the modern sense of well-disposed in thought and deed, was supposed to come naturally in kindreds.

Lear is driving hard at these traditional equivalences and expectations, turning them upside down and inside out. Cordelia's refusal to play the old dutiful kinship game by not buttering up her father marks her as un-natural, unkindly, in Elizabethan terms, though she turns out to be kind in the modern sense as the play progresses. Her sisters are at first natural and kind in Elizabethan terms, behaving as daughters were supposed to, but they quickly turn unkind in both the Elizabethan and modern senses. Behaving unnaturally, in her father's terms, provokes his disinheriting of Cordelia, which unleashes a torrent of unnatural and unkind behaviour. "Bid them farewell, Cordelia, though unkind," says France, urging natural/kind behaviour towards her unnatural/unkind father and sisters (I.i). Unkindness prevails.

Hauntingly, the grammar of France's sentence includes Cordelia herself in the unkindness, though this is nothing compared with her sisters' harshness to their old dad, their hostility to Cordelia, Edmund's malignity to his brother and his engagement in the torture of his father. Edmund, the "natural" son, claims Nature as his goddess, but actually it's the un-natural that he worships. We're made to wonder, with the Fool, what kinship means for these people: to "marvel what kin thou and thy daughters are", as he says to Lear (I.iv).

What Gloucester laments in contemporary awfulness (I.ii) is universal kindred breakdown, the collapse of natural affections:

brothers divide... the bond cracked 'twixt son and

*father... son against father. The King falls from
bias of nature – there's father against child.*

The hostile weather that engulfs Lear expresses as
it endorses the general breakdown of the natural.
The storm is *contentious* (III.iv), like the divided
kingdom. Lear eggs on this violent meteorological
disruptiveness, a sort of civil war in nature: "Blow
winds and crack your cheeks!... Crack nature's
moulds" (III.ii).

The storm out there mirrors the storm in his
mind – the dividing mind that started all the
crack-ups off. It's not the unkindness of the
elements which hurts him most, but the
unkindness of his daughters. Serve him right,
you're meant to think, for heading out on the
unkindness path. "How sharper than a serpent's
tooth it is," Lear says, "To have a thankless child"
(I.iv) – daughters worse than serpents. Goneril
has a *wolvish* look (I.iv). Only "unkind daughters"
can have caused the "subdued nature" of Edgar's
madness, Lear thinks, "pelican daughters" like
his two (III.iv) – offspring, that is, feeding, like
the mythic pelican's chicks, on the blood of their
parent (terribly negativising a traditional emblem
of Christ, the pelican mother, feeding the Church
with blood from her wounded breast).

Human nature gets denatured into the
condition of beasts like this throughout the play:
Lear is fuller, in fact, of animal imagery than any

other Shakespeare drama. Lear is out in the storm, without even a hat ("unbonnetted"), on a night when even a lion, a starving bear or ravenous wolf would take shelter (would "Keep their fur dry": III.i). He's been driven to this lower than beastly extreme through the bestialism of his daughters. They're "Tigers, not daughters", in Albany's words in his speech about Humanity preying on itself "Like monsters of the deep". They're worse than animals – even a baited bear maddened by horrid teasing would compassionately try to "lick" the tormented old man better (IV.ii). It's a worse than bestial cruelty which Lear comes terribly to think is a "Judicious punishment" on him for fathering them (III.iv).

How does Shakespeare show us a world reduced to "nothing"?

Everywhere we see a denaturing and bestialising – a negativising of humanity, goodness, and meaning. Cordelia's "Nothing, my Lord" is the starting pistol for the play's race into a world of negatives. "Nothing will come of nothing," Lear responds (I.i), and nothings exfoliate madly out of her genetic refusal.

Losses multiply. There's so much loss of life. Cordelia loses her inheritance, Lear his mind,

Gloucester his eyes. Emptied of self and sight the old men totter about the stage in a realm of zero. Lear is "an O without a figure", according to the Fool (I.iv), just a nought with no preceding number to give it value. He loses his sense of self: "Who am I?" he keeps wondering (as in I.iv). Goneril compels him to "disquantity" (diminish, reduce in number) his followers (I.iv). *Disquantity*, one of Shakespeare's most striking coinages, is the name of this play's major game: reductions of sanity, sight, things, meaning, down to nothing.

In an exercise which vividly and hauntingly performs this movement into nothingness, the sisters inexorably *scant* their father, paring his allowance of a hundred men down to none. "What need one?" is Regan's final terrible throw (II.ii). Contemporary audiences would have recognised this as an aweing parody of the scene in Genesis 18 where Abraham beats God down to the minimal number of righteous needed to save Sodom from destruction. Driven out, Lear enters the world of the poorest people with next to nothing, the "Poor naked wretches... houseless... unfed", in their clothes full of holes – "looped and windowed raggedness" (III.iv). "Off, off, you lendings," he cries, tearing at his clothes, visibly siding with ragged Edgar, the living emblem of mere humanity, the "bare, forked animal": "Unaccommodated man" (III.iv.105), the people with nothing. (This is the first recorded use of *unaccommodated*.)

"O, I have ta'en /Too little care of this," Lear says, turning the play's attention with great radical political force onto the plight of the workless and homeless, the large Elizabethan underclass with no resource but begging and crime, the horde of "masterless men" forced out onto the road by the enclosure movement.*

At the physical core of the play are overwhelming, emblematic convergences of physical absences and nothingness: Lear whose mind has gone, tearing off his clothes to join the poor and destitute; Gloucester with only empty "cases", bloody holes, for eyes (IV.vi.140); Edgar as a jabbering "nothing" ("Edgar I nothing am", II.ii.192), de-faced literally with muck, a naked "Bedlam beggar" (one of those half-cured lunatics discharged from the Bethlehem mental hospital in London with a licence to beg for a living). The Fool is a zany commentator on the real and pretend witlessness, and Kent is a sober one. ("All the power of his wits have given way," he rightly observes of Lear: III.vi.) "'Tis the time's plague when madmen lead the blind," says

*They are a major concern of the great Marxist historian of the 17th century Christopher Hill in *The World Turned Upside Down* (1972); the "unemployed" that the leftist critic Terence Hawkes, in his very good *Writers and their Work* booklet *King Lear* (1995), puts at the centre of the play's "aggravations"; down there in the depths of what the literary historian Gāmini Salgādo calls, in his 1977 classic, *The Elizabethan Underworld*. Some historians and critics think that in these social encounters and realisations Shakespeare is sharply rebuking the enormous luxury of King James's court.

Gloucester (IV.i).

There's nothing in all world literature that outdoes these central scenes for grim realisations of what human beings can be reduced to. They are as heart-stopping as those photographs of naked, skeletal concentration camp inmates at the end of the Second World War. At the heart of *Lear* we're presented with a general disease of noughting – utterly germane to which is the linguistic dissolution which fills this drama, a drama that's book-ended so awesomely by Cordelia's silent lips. Character after character follows her in saying nothing, or next to nothing.

In this play words are constantly prohibited, rebutted, denied. They keep turning into their negative, silence, or silence's near-neighbour, nonsense. "No words, no words; hush," Gloucester urges Lear, who's babbling on about Tom as a "philosopher". And this preference for silence is immediately capped by some of the most enigmatic lines in all literature, Tom's

> *Childe Rowland to the dark tower came,*
> *His word was still "Fie, foh and fum,*
> *I smell the blood of a British man". (III.v)*

"His word was still": not absolutely *still*, i.e. silent, to be sure, for Tom is *still* able to speak, which is something; but a surviving word which is *still*, i.e. persistently, incomprehensible rubbish.

Does the play undermine language itself?

The play's bitter-sweet lesson in handy-dandyism runs throughout. There is a constant aporetic stasis of opposites: justice-thief, reason-madness, sight-blindness, head-heels, poison-medicine, speech-silence, male-female.

Powering this is utter confusion about what words mean and what they actually refer to – which is all part of the play's pervasive crisis of what is known as *deixis*, the traditional power of words to point accurately *beyond* language into the world, defining the nature of things, reality,

A TRAGEDY OF LANGUAGE

"O do, de, do, de, do, de," Tom rambles (F only, III. iv): "Do, de, de, de" (III.vi in F, "loudladoodla" in Q). The favourite editorial suggestion is these *dos* and *des* are Tom's teeth chattering with cold. But why not think of them as part of the play's extraordinary roster of telling *d*-words? How hotly it mounts up, this rhetoric of the negative. Words in *di-* signal splitting and breaking, like the crucial *division* – and *divest, divulge, divide, diffidence* and *difference*. Then there are the words beginning with *dis-*, for undoing, reversing and removing, like the coinage *disquantity* – and *dissolution, disclaim, dismantle, disease, dishonour, displeasure, discommend, disposition, disnature, disorder, disordered, dissipations,*

thereness, truth. The usual deictic function of
pointing words (definite articles, demonstratives,
adverbs of location – *the, this, that, here, there*)
keeps breaking down in this play. It is repeatedly
unclear what they are pointing at. By way of
differentiating *sweet* from *bitter*, for example,
the Fool promises that

The sweet and bitter fool will presently appear,
The one in motley here, the other found out there.
                                                  (I.iv)

The *here* points to himself clearly enough, the man
in Fool's "motley" costume; but what precisely

---

displeasure, disbranch. And
the words in *de-* for
lowerings and degeneracies
of all sorts, as *deprive,*
decline, derogate, derive,
debauched, defacing,
deformity, despair. Nor can
we ignore *do-* for *dotage,*
and also Dover – that
naggingly negative place.

It all amounts to a huge
linguistic chatter of words
for failures of one sort or
another; the loud noise of
linguistic collapse: do-de-
dissonance. The deferring
of difference. Verbal
difference – the essence of

meaning in language,
according to the greatest
20th-century linguist
Ferdinand de Saussure – is
put repeatedly to the
question, long before
Jacques Derrida suggested
that difference was always,
inevitably, deferred. "Dost
know the difference, my boy,
between a bitter fool and a
sweet one?" – and Lear can
only reply "No" to the Fool's
question (I.iv). Bitter-sweet:
what's the difference?

Gender-minded critics
seize on Lear's perturbing
feminisation when he refers

does *there* indicate? It's impossible to tell: the Fool might mean Lear; he might, as Foakes's Arden note suggests, be handing over his Fool's wand, his insignia of office as Fool, to Lear, with a "there: take it". And if *there* does point to Lear as a fool, we can never be certain whether he's intended for the bitter or the sweet one. "Do you see this?... Look there, look there!" the dying Lear urges, but leaving us uncertain what *this* is, and what or where is *there*. Cordelia's lips are moving? We'll never know.

This kind of uncertainty is frequent enough in the play to indicate at the very least a serious scepticism on Shakespeare's part about language's traditional deictic power, its power fully to impart

to himself, in Act II, as suffering an *hysterica passio*, the "hysteria", known as the "mother", thought to be caused in women by upward pressure of the pregnant womb, the *hystera*. At that moment Lear can't tell the difference between fathers and mothers, female and male. What's the difference? Not being able to tell is the marker of a terrible crisis, of the self and of the language we rely on to know and speak the self and everything else. (Carol Rutter's essay "Eel Pie and Ugly Sisters in *King Lear*" dwells vividly on the way the male-female aporia runs into the speech-silence one: it's in *Lear from Study to Stage: Essays in Criticism*, ed. James Ogden & Arthur Scouten, 1997.) Truly the language of this tragedy is contriving what Russ McDonald has rightly called a "tragedy of language" ("The Language of Tragedy", in T*he Cambridge Companion to Shakespearian Tragedy*, ed Claire McEachen, 2002) ▪

meaning. "Here is the place": Kent offers Lear some shelter from the storm; "enter here"; "enter here" – F adds those two insistent *here*s (III.iv.1ff). But once again the reference of those deictic adverbs is never specified. "Here's the place" (IV.vi), Edgar tells Gloucester, pointing out the features of what he claims are Dover's cliffs, "this chalky bourn". And here the deixeis – the meanings words point to – are more than just referentially wobbly, they're downright deception and lies.

They may be lies in a good cause – Edgar charitably saving his father from suicide – but they are still lies. What's more they are special lies because they're the lies of a theatrical performance, a staged fiction, a kind of play within the play – a scene, not accidentally, that is notoriously difficult to stage convincingly. It's so "hard-to-play (because always a little hard to believe)", said the critic Geoffrey O'Brien in a review of the Royal Shakespeare Company's 2011 production of *Lear* in New York. But it's easy to take as one of Shakespeare's profoundest self-reflexive, self-referential reflections on the nature of theatre, of what he is about in this play as well as in all his work.

The Dover Cliffs episode stages what the loud, puritanical critics of theatre – enemies of the stage like Philip Stubbes in his *Anatomie of Abuses* (1583) – said all theatre was: a tissue of lies (hyper-immorality propagated, what's more, in theatres that were dens of prostitution, blasphemy, transvestism and homosexuality, cosying-up to the brothels, madhouses and prisons across the Thames in London's Southwark red-light district). But Edgar's little drama is patently a moral triumph in saving Gloucester from suicide – at the time one of the strongest of criminal actions, as well being held a major sin by all the churches.

So is Shakespeare, in effect, advising his puritan opponents that theatre can be an agent of good? That it's not simply an instrument of evil – not all like Lear's opening theatre of daughterly love-speak which goes so horribly wrong. It can get out the truth – just as the crazy theatrical arraignment of Goneril on the heath does. And as Dover offers a vision of theatre as moral instrument – Shakespeare lining up with Protestant Philip Sidney's 1595 advocacy of the moral good of tragedy against the puritans, in *A Defence of Poesie* (otherwise *An Apologie for Poetry*) – so it also mightily counteracts the linguistic negativities, the deictic difficulties, which it stages. Amidst the pronounced linguistic fecklessness comes the moral positive of Edgar's goodness, his staunchness – the loyalty of a child and a son – shining bright, like Kent's loyalty and Cordelia's love, against the dark backcloth of what Kent calls "this tough world" (V.iii).

And something positive does keep emerging, like this, through the pronounced negations of word-power. The word keeps being undermined, driven into blur, gibberish, and actual silence; but silence, *Lear* suggests, has its eloquence, beginning with Cordelia's refusals which, as the cliché has it, speak volumes. The wicked are awfully eloquent – witness Lear's torrential curses, the "glib" tongues of Goneril and Regan, Edmund's tongue-twister brilliance – and thus, by contrast, Cordelia's silences acquire moral force per se.

This moral force of silence is parodied in Edmund's play with the pretend letter from Edgar: it means the more, the more it is withheld – like the absent handkerchief in *Othello*, loaded with meaning by treacherous Iago, Edmund's word-brilliant brother in crime. "The quality of nothing hath not such need to hide itself. Let's see. – Come, if it be nothing, I shall not need spectacles," as Gloucester explains (I.ii).

There's nothing more compelling, more moving, more feelingly truthful, neither in this play nor in all of world literature, than Lear's heavy negatives, his *O*s and *no*s and *never*s: here's the overwhelming revelatory force, the eloquence, that comes of being irredeemably installed into Cordelia's silenced ethos, the world of the unheard and unutterable, of language disaster.

What is't thou sayst? Her voice was ever soft,

Gentle and low, an excellent thing in woman.
(V.iii)

This is not to be thought of as some sort of anti-woman, unfeminist, slight, but a haunting recall of the genesis of Lear's downfall when he urged loquacity on his daughters. Silence, linguistic withdrawals, gaps, hollows, do have their considerable power, their truth, however horribly exemplified in the silence of his beloved daughter's death. Devastating silence, in fact, is all Lear is left with; it's what we are all made to share with him. Nothing in literature has more power than the expression, in Lear's final words, of the powerlessness of the word: "Look there!" Here, so eloquently expressed, is the ultimate impotence of the deictic will. It's what rivets every audience – and makes for as good a definition as any, perhaps, of "tragedy" itself.

How sympathetic is Shakespeare's treatment of women in *Lear*?

Feminist critics argue that everything in the play should be seen from the perspective of its women – its daughters, sisters, wives, mothers, whores. This feminising and genderising of *Lear*, as of other Shakespeare plays, is a lively fulfilment of

Virginia Woolf's challenge, in A *Room of One's Own* (1929), to imagine Shakespeare having a sister – Woolf called her Judith – who would write plays but fail to get them staged in London's male theatrical world. Woolf's point is that Judith should be allowed to speak out, and feminist criticism has, in effect, let her do so.

The rock duo "Shakespeare's Sister" got Woolf's point; so has the sisterhood of Shakespeare critics. *Lear* "is not the play of the king but of the daughters", says Carol Rutter characteristically. It's a "daughter play". And it's through the daughters that the play's big questions of language are explored: what speaking out entails; what it means "to say 'Nothing'"; how metaphors perform or not.

> I want to notice... the way in [Shakespeare's] theatre (where language is not just iterative, but creative, where words work like God's, to realize, to materialize) the metaphors men speak, women play out.

So Hamlet feigns madness, Ophelia goes mad; Macbeth murders sleep, Lady Macbeth sleepwalks; Leontes hardens his heart, Hermione turns to stone. It is the same in *Lear*. "Lear makes the metaphors of this play; Goneril and Regan literalize them... He makes his daughters monstrous. They grow monstrous."

Speaking up for the women often results in sympathy for the wicked sisters, especially Goneril. Feminist critics approve of the 1962 Peter Brook production where the extremely rowdy knights made Goneril's anger understandable. It's a convention, in fact, of feminist critique that the bad sisters need finer understanding than they used to get, being greatly sinned against as well as sinning – and Cordelia having always been

HYSTERICA PASSIO

Lear's reaction in II.ii at finding Kent put in the stocks by Cornwall and Goneril – instantly blamed in his misogynistic fashion on "this daughter" – is, startlingly, what he and his time thought of as womanly hysteria:

O, how this mother swells up
toward my heart!
Hysterica passio, down, thou
climbing sorrow,
Thy element's below. (II.ii)

Hysterica passio – "emotion of the womb" (Greek hystera = womb) – got its name from its alleged cause, the pregnant womb pushing up painfully against the heart, the seat of the emotions. As the emotional distress of pregnant women, it was known as "the mother". (Hysteria was traditionally considered the over-emotionality special to humans with wombs.) So what is Shakespeare doing in turning Lear's daughter-induced distress into the disease of a pregnant woman?

For the feminist psychoanalytical critic Coppélia Kahn, the play is a representative "tragedy" of a grown-up male cut off from his womb-mother and desiring a maternal substitute

preferred by their father.

Such sympathy began, more or less, with the foundational modern feminising work, Juliet Dusinberre's 1975 *Shakespeare and the Nature of Women*. You have to acknowledge, she argues, the monstrosity, the deformity of Goneril and Regan, but qualify it: "Cornwall's violence is as vile as Regan's, more vile than Goneril's." Goneril's violence is not so bad because it "only takes the

in a daughter. Lear's "madness is essentially his rage at being deprived of the maternal presence". The hysterical "mother" is the return of the traumatically repressed mother, a repression played out in the complete absence of real mothers from the *Lear* stage – though why this return should seem a marker of continuing distress rather than otherwise is not explained.

Much more plausible is to take Lear's "mother" moment as part of the play's repeated unsettling of gender identities and roles – a blurring of gender boundaries consistent with the play's huge repertoire of disconcerting handy-dandy (what's-the-difference?) blurrings. Lear hates being effeminised, as he thinks, by shedding tears: he's "ashamed" that Goneril has power "to shake my manhood" by inducing "hot tears" (I.iv). When the "mother" strikes again, Lear tries to subdue it, crying "My rising heart!... down!" – a resistance the Fool urges on in a frenzy of gender topsy-turvydom, likening Lear to a cockney woman pastry-cook bashing eels on the head to fit them into her pie, and crying "Down, wantons, down!"

Carol Rutter is one exuberant celebrator of the gender challenge symptomatised in the hysterica passio and in Lear's playing "a female domestic, a mad lady pastry chef". (With

form of poisoning her sister and stabbing herself". (*Only!!*)

Dusinberre's pitch is that Shakespeare's plays were naturally feminist because of the large number of women in the audience, but also because Protestant-Puritan London was feminist. Cordelia's keeping silent on her own terms should be seen as a *resistance* to the old Biblical tradition that women should be submissive to men and

---

lovely phrases like that, it's no surprise that one of Rutter's workshops turned comedian Lenny Henry's school-induced Shakespeare-phobia into enthusiasm, and got him going as a serious Shakespearian actor.) But Rutter's caution about Lear's effeminisation also seems wise. There is indeed a kind of "tragedy" in this "deterioration of the masculine"; and Rutter has force in suggesting it's "an appalling act of cultural aggression that – even as he makes his daughters male monsters, Centaurs, and himself "the mother" – perverts the feminine and occupies the feminine space to wreck it".

Rutter's careful label for the play's gender inversions is *catachresis*, the old name for a rhetoric of perversion and distortion. It's a set of inversions which, as the always canny Patricia Parker argues, the Fool apparently suggests is an extended play of the preposterous. This is when in I.iv the Fool berates Lear for acts of self-infantilising and effeminising which have perverted the standard relation of father and daughters.

Lear has made his daughters his mothers – as it were pulling down his own trousers, baring his bottom, and giving them the stick to beat him with; Goneril's hostility to him over the knights' behaviour is like a cuckoo biting off the head of

express that submission in silence – a choosiness Dusinberre's thinks London's Puritan preachers would approve of. Shakespeare is "realistic" about family life because Puritan sermons on home-life provided him with "raw material for plays no longer devoted to life as it ought to be in defiance of life as it is".

Dusinberre's Puritan detail is dodgy, and sometimes plain wrong, but that matters less than

---

the hedge-sparrow that's fed it. Things are all back to front; as any fool can see. "May not an ass" – or fool – "know when the cart draws the horse?" Getting things back to front like that is a disorder of speech and logic known in ancient rhetoric books as *hysteron proteron*.

In the great contemporary work by George Puttenham, *The Arte of English Poesie* (1589), which translates the Greek and Roman rhetorical terms for women, who haven't Greek and Latin, *hysteron proteron* is Englished as *the Preposterous*, with the proverb "the cart before the horse" as prime example. Patricia Parker points out that preposterous is

Shakespeare's usual word for the inversions, reversals and disorders of society, hierarchy, family, selfhood, sexuality, that his plays keep investigating. *Hysteron proteron* – "what's behind (Greek *hysteros*) placed foremost" – has nothing etymologically to do with *hystera*, womb, and Lear's *hysterica*, but it's arrestingly linked to them by rhyme. A rhyming link seemingly heard by the Fool. And if he is indeed suggesting Lear's mothering is preposterous, then that means he thinks it "contrary to nature, reason or commonsense; monstrous; foolish, perverse" (Oxford English Dictionary). Which would seem to be what Lear himself thinks ∎

her influential big picture of Shakespeare foregrounding questions of woman's nature, place, and role; and his engaging in contemporary discussions of family and marriage not as done deals but as matters for continuing argument and imaginative probing. Dusinberre it was who opened up the question of why the mothers of the sisters and of Edgar and Edmund are all absent, denied presence and voice. After Dusinberre, no one would take for granted Lear's monstrous patriarchalism and misogyny, or Gloucester's cheerful bad behaviour as husband and lover, or the old couple's awfulness as fathers; and Goneril would be sympathised with, and the saintliness of Cordelia would be chipped away at. And of course the blurring of conventional gender differences, Lear's "mothering" and all that, would be taken as utterly central to the play's anxious consideration of human nature and selfhood.

And strong, challenging feminist readings were soon pouring through the floodgate that Dusinberre opened. According to Lynda E. Boose's in "The Father and the Bride in Shakespeare" (1982), Shakespeare's plays are highly emotional dramas about families – they "consistently explore affective family dynamics with an intensity that justifies the inference... that the plays may be

Opposite: Sylvester McCoy as the Fool in Trevor Nunn's much-lauded Royal Shakespeare Company production, 2007. In a twist on the text, the Fool was hanged on stage.

primarily 'about' family relations and only secondarily about the macrocosm of the body politic" – with an emphasis on the fraught relation of daughters to fathers.

On this view, Lear arranges a grotesque, parodic marriage ceremony for Cordelia, one carefully designed to prevent her being handed over in orthodox fashion in marriage to another man (the offered "dowry" is a curse), because he wants to keep her incestuously for himself. Lear and Cordelia's late reunion is the start of a long desired renewal of the old "incestuous proximity" of father and unmarried daughter (two love-birds in the cage with husband France well out of the way). The play ends in wholesale family death – of the father and his three daughters – as it must in a family tragedy doomed from the start by the father's refusal to play a father's proper part. The "cost demanded of the daughter is appallingly high".

The Freudianism is, of course, greatly over-done, infantilised oedipalism piled on to the alleged incestuous desire. Reunited with his daughter at the last, Lear thinks he is going to enjoy the "kind nursery" of Cordelia which he craved at the start (II.i) – as an infant feeding at his daughter's breast.

But that's a terrible misreading of "kind nursery", which is in reality more a vision of Cordelia's abode as a sort of Private Care Home for the Elderly rather than a desired return to the breast. This, however, hasn't stopped the mistake catching on, and feeding the likes of Coppélia Kahn's ultra-Freudian take, in her 1986 piece "The Absent Mother in *King Lear*". It's the missing breast that drives Lear mad, thinks Kahn, and afflicts him with "the mother". The *hysterica passio* he talks of "is a searing sense of loss at the deprivation of the mother's presence": "In Freud's unforgettable phrase, he is 'his majesty, the baby'." Not having Cordelia's breast in his mouth causes Lear's "oral rage" – the bad-mouthing of Goneril; his fantasy of gorging his appetite on his wicked offspring and being eaten by his "pelican" daughters.

It would be a pity if all this loose-cannon Freudianism distracted from what is perhaps the greatest force of feminist critique of *Lear*, namely its affirmation of the play's pivotal concern with bodies. "Produce the bodies," Albany commands (V.iii), and *Lear* keeps producing the body as subject. Every production is, in a sense, a *body*-production – about what the body, human flesh, might mean. The bodies are of both genders, but the play is book-ended by women's bodies, for we begin with Gloucester's feisty recall of Edmund's "round-wombed" mother, and end with Cordelia's corpse.

Lear is fascinated by the flesh, his own and other people's: the flesh which "begot" his daughters (III.iv); the "bare forked animal" Edgar/Tom; the "Poor naked wretches" of his kingdom. Tom's "presented nakedness" troubles him mightily: how terrible if the body, so weak and vulnerable, so easily ruined and destroyed, so mortal, were the essence of the human, were the "thing itself". "Is man no more than this?" (III.iv). Hamlet has his flesh worries, too, but for him there's much more to "a man" than the body: the human essence is rather "godlike reason", and there is some sort of life after death. Lear has no such consolations; the body is absolute, and that's a paining thought because the body in this play is the zone of perpetual sado-masochistic attention.

Lear, in the Fool's metaphor, has masochistically pulled down his own trousers and given his daughters the rod to beat him with (I.iv). Male masochism meets female sadism – the sadism manifest most horribly in Regan's gloating participation in Gloucester's blinding, Cornwall's

Out, vile jelly,
Where is thy lustre now? (III.vii)

But one horrible irony of *Lear* is that this gouging out of Gloucester's eyes, the piercing of his body, being left with bloody holes for eyes, is the way to insight. This way he finds out the truth of Edgar's "abuse": he's enriched, he says, by new possessions ("commodities") of knowledge (IV.i). And the disconcerting way that the punctured body of the male is the gateway to insight is replicated when the boot is on the other gender foot. Beadles, local constables, lash the stripped bodies of prostitutes for their fleshy transgressions, but Lear on the heath comes to see that they should themselves be stripped and whipped for their "'hotly lusting" after those women. The small bodily "vices" of the poor are visible through the holes in their clothes; the "Robes and furred gowns" of the rich conceal their massively bad bodies. So the play's handy-dandy truths about ethics, class and gender, depend, apparently, on such body exposures and hurtings.

Lear would have Regan *anatomized* – cut open in a fiendish surgical examination, for the truth of her wicked heart to be exposed (III.vi). The thought of truth-finding on this body cut-up plan is all one with Lear in body-hating, sado-masochistic curse mode in I.iv. Because of her hostility to his knights, Nature must invade Goneril's womb and "convey" sterility there: terrible negative impregnation by rape. If she have a child it must cause her violent body damage: "stamp wrinkles" on her forehead, cause weeping that will cut ("fret") *channels* in her cheeks. Lear's thought of his curses as malign incestuous desire immediately prompts a sado-masochistic flurry: his masochistic claim that he'll pluck out his own "old fond" eyes if Goneril makes him weep again, and the sadistic hope that Regan will "flay" her sister's "wolvish" face when she hears of Goneril's hostility.

The audience of Elizabethan and Jacobean

THE CRITICS ON *LEAR*

In Lear *Shakespeare "makes no just distribution of good and evil".*

Dr Samuel Johnson,
Preface to his edition of Shakespeare's Works, 1765

Requital, redemption, amends, equity, explanation, pity and mercy, are words without a meaning here.

Algernon Charles Swinburne,
A Study of Shakespeare, 1880

When I read Shakespeare I am struck with wonder that such trivial people should muse and thunder in such lovely language.

D.H. Lawrence, "When I Read Shakespeare",
Pansies: Poems, 1929

Shakespeare was "noticeably cautious, not to say cowardly, in his manner of uttering unpopular opinions... Throughout his plays, the acute social critics, the people who are not taken in by accepted fallacies, are buffoons, villains, lunatics or persons who are shamming insanity or in a state of violent hysteria."

George Orwell, "Lear, Tolstoy and the Fool", 1947

Achieved art is quite incapable of lowering the spirits. If this were not so, each performance of

King Lear would end in a Jonestown. [Jonestown, Guyana: site of the mass suicide of a sectarian Christian group, 1978].

Martin Amis, Introduction to his *Selection of Philip Larkin's Poems*, 2011

In King Lear *[Shakespeare] starts from the hypothesis...that the gods are indifferent, or hostile, or inexplicable, or even a man-made fiction, and that there is no after-life in which the injustices of life on earth may be set right.*

Kenneth Muir, *Penguin Critical Studies: King Lear* (1986)

Cordelia's hanging and Gloucester's blinding are proof of "the willful operations of an upside down providence in an apparently deranged universe".

W. R. Elton, *King Lear and the Gods*, 1966

[A. C.] Bradley, with that readiness to admit spiritual resonance that our age too curtly dismisses as absurd, rightly identified a quasi-transcendent moral music in the play. This music is set against the almost unrelieved pain of the practical sequence... At the end of the play we are not sure that Cordelia is in heaven, but unless we are entirely brutalized, we do feel that we have glimpsed, beyond the chaotic horror, something of infinite sweetness that we cannot fully comprehend.

A. D. Nuttall, *Shakespeare the Thinker*, 2007

drama liked a big body-count at the end, and *King Lear* comes well up to scratch. When Albany orders "Produce the bodies", the corpses of Goneril and Regan are immediately carried in. This play is a body-production all right; and a *dead*-body production what's more; with Albany as its belated stage-manager. Soon after the production of the dead sisters, Albany commands dead Edmund "borne hence", which is followed by Lear coming in carrying dead Cordelia. Very soon after that, Albany orders the bodies of Cordelia and Regan "borne hence". With dead Lear, that's five dead bodies at the end; two male, and three female – a female body prominence that Carol Rutter wants to read as a continuation of the play's woman-centredness. *Enter the Body* is the title of her powerful 2001 book about woman as Shakespeare's main preoccupation. "Enter the body": it's all at once a stage direction, and a description of what happens in the play, as well as a nod to the sexual penetrations the play keeps talking about.

The play's main challenge for Rutter is to make sense of all the bodily material, especially the body gendered as female (which includes "mothered" Lear), a problem that climaxes in Lear's difficulty in reading the "dead silent" body of Cordelia at the end. So the play's great concern with meaning is most forcefully focused – as feminist criticism thinks it should be – on the female subject. It is focused, too, on Cordelia as a main addition to the group of dead females whom Rutter describes as the Tragedies' "signs or symbols": Desdemona, Ophelia, Lady Macbeth.

Where does *Lear* leave us in the end?

Desire for some great effect and affect, for strong tangible meanings to take away at the end of a performance or reading, has hung heavy over the great potent fictions known as tragedies ever since Aristotle in his *Poetics* said that the audience's experience of the characters' learning processes, their growth in knowledge and self-knowledge, should result in *catharsis*, the purging, the cleaning out, of the strong emotions these narratives had evoked – pity and terror and "such emotions". The outcome which, in his adaptation of *catharsis* in a Latin epigraph to his tragedy *Samson Agonistes* (1671), John Milton called *lustration* – cleansing as through a process of sacrificial religious ritual. And this traditional expectation of our ending up emotionally and thus morally bettered, certainly wiser, because armed at the end with important truths the tragedy has uncovered – revelations, literally *apocalypses* – has attached with particular force to this greatest of all tragedies.

Stephen Booth has dwelt rather mockingly, in "On the Greatness of *King Lear*", on "our all-but-desperate need to believe that Lear learns something between Act I and his death, and the solemn vigour with which critics will fix on (and demand that the play be midwife to) a single pregnant phrase like 'Ripeness is all'". But engaging with end truths, something memorable for us at the end, is what *Lear* does a lot. It's massively preoccupied with ends. Ending up is in contention right from the start when Lear gives up his kingdom so he can "Unburdened crawl toward death" (I.i).

"Yours in the ranks of death," Edmund promises Goneril when he goes off to fight against Cordelia's troops (IV.ii). Everyone in this play is in death's army. Agonised Gloucester wants to die: "let me die"; "Is wretchedness deprived that benefit/ To end itself by death?" (IV.vi). Lear tells a Gentleman "I will die bravely, like a smug bridegroom" (IV.vi). Fear of dying drives Edgar into the living death of poverty:

> *O, our lives' sweetness,*
> *That we the pain of death would hourly die*
> *Rather than die at once! (V.iii)*

Personal end-times preoccupy, but so does the grand and final end-time when final end-truths will be learned, the Last Day of "Doom", Judgement, Reckoning, on the last day or page of history, as promised and prophesied in the Biblical

Grand Narrative of history. This story climaxes in the last book of the Bible, The Book of Revelation, the Apocalypse, when the Divine Judge does justice, distinguishing the good sheep from the wicked goats, apportioning praise and blame, handing out rewards and punishments, heaven for the good, hell for the bad.

"Is this the promised end?" Kent wonders, in the play's dying moments as Lear enters carrying the dead Cordelia. It seems to him that the Final Judgement Day might have arrived, in this play which keeps feeling apocalyptic, offering so much momentous revelation about the most serious matters. Stephen Booth is wrong to mock. The play's potency consists precisely in the imposing impact of its admittedly awful revelations. *King Lear* is a horror story – a play full of horror stories, lessons in negativities of all sorts, revelations about the propensity of humans to inhumanity, wickedness and cruelty, bestialism even, to evil by any reckoning.

Lear is about the ease with which power segues into tyranny, the speed with which reigns of terror begin and take off, the unkindness which reigns where kindness might be expected to be most manifest – among kindred, in families. It is full, in short, of revelations about the moral fragilities of human nature – its true unnaturalness, as one might say. The moral frailties run up and down the generations.

> When Edgar says of Lear, "He childed as I father'd", the tragedy is condensed into just five words.

That's the critic Harold Bloom in old age, in *Shakespeare: The Invention of the Human*, quite "startled" by Lear as a "terrible emblem of fatherhood itself". "*Ein alter Mann ist stets ein König Lear*" – an old man is always a King Lear – thus Goethe when he too was in old age. This terrible conviction is one carried away from the play by many an aged critic and director, like Ingmar Bergman, the film-maker, who directed the famously apocalyptic 1983 Swedish stage production of *Lear*. (It finished with a series of world-ending military explosions.) The composer Alexander Goehr, at the age of 78, also thought old age the key to the play: "As an incipient old man myself that's what interested me." He titled his *Lear* opera *Promised End*; it was his swansong, he said.

The play makes these old witnesses feel with dismay that Lear is a case of Everyman in old age, of all old men as deplorable patriarchs. But neither does it spare younger generations, for it seems to grant Goneril, Regan and Edmund representative status as what sons and daughters can easily be. "How sharper than a serpent's tooth it is/To have thankless child," says Lear (I.iv). And ingratitude, it's suggested, is par for the course with the class of younger humans.

Ethical negativity, then – everywhere – is this play's constant point. In its society, the wretched poor all go naked and homeless, their plight acknowledged, under duress, by the powers-that-be, but completely unalleviated in practice. Justice – legal order – is invoked but seems quite out of kilter. In effect there's no moral order either. "When the bad bleed, then is the tragedy good," declares the revenger Vindice in Middleton's *The Revenger's Tragedy* (1607), a close contemporary of *Lear*. In *Lear*, though, the good and the bad all bleed, literally as well as metaphorically – the good Cordelia along with the bad Oswald, Edmund, Goneril, Regan, and the dodgy Lear and Gloucester.

Gods of all sorts are invoked but to no agreed effect. The Biblical Grand Narrative of redemption through suffering and scapegoating is alluded to, but not wholeheartedly performed. There are indeed changes of heart, but Lear's does nothing for the poor, and Edmund's comes too late to save Cordelia. Contingency and randomness reign: Cordelia's death is just one of life's horrible accidents.

And philosophical confusion goes along with the moral and metaphysical chaos. Philosophical confidence is massively lacking. What is wisdom, the play asks, that goal of philosophy from ancient times? What is reason, that necessary instrument of thought? Our grip on reality, and ability to interpret it, are constantly called into question, with dismal results for the very idea of knowledge and self-knowledge seeming inevitable in the large dramatic collapse of language, the word's slither into dubious referentialism, gibberish, nothingness.

So how does *Lear* look forward to Beckett and the Theatre of the Absurd?

So negativity is piled upon negativity; there is emptying, devastation, lack, all round. Harold Bloom is quite right to invoke *kenoma* as the play's endgame, kenoma being the condition of spiritual emptiness in Gnostic philosophy (that ancient Christianising of Greek thought).

The emptying-out of positives in this play has indeed been hard to accept. It drove the Nahum Tate rewrite and maintained its long popularity. Most modern productions, on the other hand, have rather welcomed the emptying-out as anticipating 20th-century patriarchal totalitarianism, existential angst, humanist bleakness, absurdism. They embrace the Shakespeare who, as the Polish critic Jan Kott famously put it, is overwhelmingly Our Contemporary (*Shakespeare Our Contemporary*, 1964).

Jan Kott, survivor of mid-20th-century horrors, veteran of the Polish Underground in the Second

World War and acquainted first-hand with later Stalinist repression, is backed by Peter Brook, in his Preface to the 1967 English revised edition of Kott's book, as

> undoubtedly the only writer on Elizabethan matters who assumes without question that every one of his readers will at some point or other have been woken by the police in the middle of the night... Shakespeare is a contemporary of Kott, Kott is a contemporary of Shakespeare.

Feeling some such contemporary political force is presumably what drove the Jewish Kulturbund of Berlin to put on Samuel Halkin's Yiddish translation in the 1930s. It was no doubt the terror subject, combined with an arresting interest in the play's suggestion of divine indifference to suffering – that great preoccupation of orthodox Jewish writing and thought in the Hitler period – which drove the German-Jewish dentist Abraham Asen to make a Yiddish translation in the Bergen-Belsen concentration camp.*

Jan Kott gives us a *Lear* proleptically eloquent against the theory and practice of Sovietised

*It's utterly fitting, as it were, that Samuel Micoyels, the veteran thirties Yiddish Lear, who played the king in his Troupe's production of Asen's translation in Stalinist Moscow after the Second World War, should have been mysteriously run over and killed on a Moscow Street in 1948, and all his Troupe eliminated.

Eastern Bloc Marxism. The play, he writes, rejects the "rational view of history" – he means especially Marxism – and socialist utopianism: it

> makes a tragic mockery of all eschatologies: of the heaven promised on earth, and the heaven promised hereafter; in fact – of both Christian and secular theodicies.

Kott is thinking in particular of the desired end of revolutionary heavens on earth – secular pastiche of Christian heavenly endedness. *The Endgame of Lear*, as Kott keeps calling it, after Samuel Beckett's play of 1959, is quite otherwise. The narrative of Kott's *Lear* is Absurdist, absolutely opposite to the purposeful Christian Grand Narrative and its Marxist offspring. It is utterly Beckettian – as was Peter Brook's 1962 production (still offered by critics as a Kottian endeavour, whereas it preceded Kott's book by some years, and was driven independently by Beckett's influence).

Kott's reading – and Brook's too – is well-judged, for Beckett's numerous, increasingly stripped-down texts of *néant* – nothingness, or absence – draw their sap and substance from Lear's emptyings. Beckett's humanity, as it's put in his most famous play, *Waiting for Godot* (1954), is "born astride" of a sound-alike Lear-type grave. The death-bound new-born's cry is the only event in the miniscule *Breath* (1969), all at once the noise of a birth and a death – a meaningless birth into "this great stage of fools", as Lear puts it. Instead of the gods of *Lear*, the scene in Beckett's most famous play is haunted by Godot, a saviour and meaning-supplier, whose arrival and Last Day are eagerly awaited but endlessly deferred. Blind Hamm in his wheel-chair in *Endgame*, going nowhere much, is an all-in-one reprise of Gloucester and Lear.

Paralysis and doubt – or aporia – are pretty universal conditions in Beckett. His people are a bunch of disabled pilgrims, stuck, or at least hampered, en route to their destined end. It's a *Lear*-inspired impededness dramatised at the start of *Godot*, where Estragon, foot hurting, tries to take his boot off and find what the problem is.

"Help me off with this bloody thing," he demands of Vladimir, turning the vague deixeis of *Lear* to comic effect, as he points at Vladimir's unbuttoned flies. Vladimir buttons up ("Never neglect the little things of life"). Boot finally off, Estragon finds "Nothing" in it, but he still "airs" it. "There's man all over for you. Blaming on his boots the faults of his feet," says Vladimir.

This boots-button play is the prelude in *Godot* to intense worries about salvation and repentance and the point of life. What is "Our being born" for, wonders Estragon. All of which is a paying of dues to *Lear*. Estragon is mimicking Lear's getting Gloucester to pull off his boots ("harder, harder, so") – which drove Edgar to his "matter and impertinency mixed,/Reason in madness" observation and led into Lear's sermon on our wawling and crying "the first time we smell the air"' of "this great stage of fools". Beckett's drama of undone boots is wrapped around his mocking fly-button update of Lear's fetish about undone buttons: "unbutton here", Lear demands on the heath (III.iv), and, later, "Pray you undo this button" – his own or Cordelia's: yet one more deictic blur (V.iii).

Grand Lear has to learn to mind the little things of life, learn the importance of hurtful matter, take in the force, in the end, of emptiness – emptied boots, emptied life. And it is the little things, next-to-nothings, actual nothings, which Beckett makes resound as he follows in the pained footsteps of *Lear*. He's upsettingly mindful, for example, of the scene where mad Edgar leads blind Gloucester on the Dover road – that moving take on Jesus's words about the Pharisees: "And if the blind lead the blind, both shall fall into the ditch" (Matthew 15.14).

When he wrote *Godot,* Beckett was doubtless recalling not only Lear's Dover Road picture of human degradation and needy suffering, but also that terrifying 1558 painting by Pieter Breughel the Elder of a row of five blind beggars being led along a precipitous edge by a sixth one. (Breughel's paintings are often invoked by critics as parallels to Shakespeare's fictions, and so they can be, though there's no evidence that Shakespeare actually knew his great contemporary's work.) "About suffering they were never wrong,/The Old Masters," said W.H. Auden in his 1938 poem "Musée des Beaux Arts", meditating on Breughel's painting of the Fall of Icarus. And Beckett plainly thought Shakespeare the Old Master was right enough about suffering to want to keep re-doing and re-voicing his awful endgames of deprivation and loss. (*Modern Shakespeare Offshoots*, 1976, by Beckett expert Ruby Cohn, is first port of call for the story of Beckett's *Lear* redoings.)

What's striking, though, about Beckett's replay of *Lear*'s endgames is that they are never finally played out. Beckett's people and Beckett's texts – both of them *Lear*'s offspring – are horrified apocalyptics, forever on their way to some end; but they never quite get there. Going over into utter nothingness is in the end endlessly deferred. They head towards the worst, look the worst in the face, experience what feels to them like the worst by way of pain – physical, spiritual, ontological, epistemic. *Worstward Ho* is their cry (in the words of Beckett's 1983 title). But the anticipated worst of utter silence never actually eventuates. *Worstward Ho* ends, characteristically: "Said nohow on". Nohow can saying go on; but still the no-saying persists. Closure, finality, are announced but don't quite happen; nearly, but not quite. "You must go on, I can't go on, I'll go on" are the famous last words of Beckett's novel *The Unnameable* (1953). Which is, you might say, aporia-lite; there's always a kind of light at the end of Beckett's aporetic tunnel. And this final deferring of the end at the end is also what Beckett gets from *Lear*.

Lear's gaze is perpetually turned worst-wards. And what's felt to be the worst keeps arriving, but never as absolutely as that superlative purports to announce. Edgar in Bedlam-beggar mode in IV.i thinks he's experiencing "the worst" that the socially and economically wretched know, but the sight of blind Gloucester offers him worse.

> *O gods! Who is't can say "I am at the worst"?*
> *I am worse than e'er I was. (IV.i.27-8)*

And being identified as "poor mad Tom" by an Old Man spurs some reflection of a very "Said nohow on" Beckettian kind about the worst not happening so long as you can still talk about it:

> *And worse I may be yet; the worst is not*
> *So long as we can say "This is the worst". (29-30)*

The worst that can be comes – yet it is still to come. Which is not unlike Lear's madness and the deaths of Cordelia and Lear, all at once arrived, but still awaited. At least, it's simply impossible to tell when exactly Lear's much anticipated madness sets in.

O let me not be mad, not mad, sweet heaven! I would not be mad. Keep me in temper, I would not be mad. (I.v.43-5)

Now, I prithee, daughter do not make me mad. (II.ii.407)

O fool, I shall go mad. (II.ii.475)

My wits begin to turn. (III.ii.67)

O, that way madness lies. (III.iv.21)

It's always coming, and we assume arrives, but we don't know when. The time of Cordelia's death is likewise fogged. "She's dead as earth," Lear firmly declares, but still wants a mirror to see whether she's still breathing (V.iii.259), and 50 lines later he's urging the others to look at her lips, apparently thinking she's still alive.

His own death date is murky too. "He dies," a stage direction insists (V.ii, though only in F). Edgar thinks "he faints". "Break, heart, I prithee break," says Kent, apparently in grief at his master's demise; but only in F – in Q these are Lear's own words, urging death on himself. Edgar, in F, then exhorts Lear to "look up", prompting Kent to tell him to let Lear "pass":

> *He hates him*
> *That would upon the rack of this tough world*
> *Stretch him out longer. (V.iii.312-14)*

Madness and death: both are so painfully stretched out. As Regan unkindly put it to her father:

> *you are old:*
> *Nature in you stands on the very verge*
> *Of her confine. (II.ii)*

From the start he's on the verge of death, that extremity, and he is perched there for most of the play; to be sure, he's finally tipped over that verge, as he was into madness, but his hovering on the threshold of the extreme, of the worst, of a close and closure, does blur that arrival. Like being on the Dover Road, and getting there, or not quite, it is all very Beckettian as it is Derridean and handydandyish.

"[D]rive toward Dover, friend": the still sighted Gloucester urges Kent to follow him there, and to take Lear along (III.vi). Dover is where Cordelia and the French army are, but it is also a potent emblem of the edge, the verge, the extreme condition towards which the play drives, and at which it keeps, in many ways, actually arriving. It is a place of dissolution, the "chalky bourn" – i.e. border – of England, in Edgar's words (IV.vi), referring to Dover's white cliffs, but pointedly using Hamlet's word for the border between life and death, the "bourn" of "the undiscovered country" from which "No traveller returns" (*Hamlet* III.i.79-80).

Dover is a destination arrived at, but with a Beckettian not-quite-ness about it: the "extreme verge" to which Edgar is leading, and actually misleading, the suicidal Gloucester:

> *Give me your hand: you are now within a foot*
> *Of th'extreme verge. (IV.vi)*

Gloucester is there, but, crucially, not quite there. He's a single footstep away; which makes a huge difference. Uncannily, as Jacques Derrida would observe, the mere naming of that place negates its extremity, at least in the linguistic endgame of Derrida's French, where the word *pas*, a footstep, also means *not*. Gloucester experiences the extremity of the verge yet doesn't experience it. Death will really come later, but for now it is imagined death that he goes through. And we, the audience of this drama, experience this imagined death too, driven, as we are, to live through extreme horrors – but by proxy, at second-hand, in the imagination.

"Is this the promised end?" Kent's question invites a Yes and No answer. The endlessly promised end has come; it does come, but peculiarly, for it keeps coming as Edgar's qualification – "Or image of that horror?" – indicates. Here is the reality of apocalyptic bad-endedness, of worstness and worstnesses – but it's an *imagined* real; true, awfully true, but *fictional* truth, the truth of very extreme fiction – of tragedy no less.

A SHORT CHRONOLOGY

1140 Oldest written reference to King Lear (spelt "Leir") provided by George Monmouth in *History of the English Kings* which describes him as a pre-Christian warrior king in what is now south-west England.

1564 Shakespeare born in Stratford-upon-Avon.

1603-1606 *King Lear* written.

1606 December 26 Only recorded performance of *King Lear* during Shakespeare's lifetime. It is generally thought that Richard Burbage played King Lear, John Hemmings was Gloucester, and Robert Armin played the Fool.

1608 Shakespeare's earlier version of *King Lear, The True Chronicle Historie of King Leir and His Three Daughters* published in quarto.

1608 Shakespeare's friend and fellow actor, Richard Burbage, inherited the Blackfriars Theatre upon the death of his father. Richard Burbage, his brother, and four of the King's Men, including Shakespeare, became part-owners in the theatre.

1616 April 23 Shakespeare dies.

1623 *The Tragedie of King Lear* published in folio.

1681 Nahum Tate's version of *King Lear* which has a happy ending in which Lear survives and triumphs, Edgar and Cordelia get married and the Fool is entirely omitted. It holds the stage until 1838.

1838 William Charles Macready brings back the original Shakespeare version of *King Lear* and has the fool played by an actress, Priscilla Horton.

1946 Laurence Olivier plays *King Lear* in a performance at the Old Vic.

1962 Fabled "Beckettian" production of *King Lear* by Peter Brook for the Royal Shakespeare Company.

1976 Trevor Nunn directs a production of *King Lear* featuring Donald Sinden as Lear and Judi Dench as Regan.

1997 Stanford University Press publish Sigmund Freud's *Writings on Art and Literature* in which Freud asserts that Cordelia symbolises Death. In the play's ending scene when Lear carries in the body of Cordelia, she causes a realisation in Lear of his finitude; she causes him to "make friends with the necessity of dying".

THE DIFFERENT VERSIONS
OF *KING LEAR*

In 1986, after hundreds of years of conflated texts whose construction largely depended on editors' whims, Stanley Wells and Gary Taylor, the editors of the *Oxford Complete Works of Shakespeare*, broke with tradition. They accepted it was wrong to go on pretending that the two main versions of the play – *The True Chronicle History of King Leir, and his three daughters, Gonerill, Ragan, and Cordilla*, published as a Quarto volume in 1608 (Q), and *The Tragedy of King Lear*, published in the later 1623 Folio collection of Shakespeare's plays (F) – were not quite separate. So they published the two versions side by side in their *Complete Works*.

There's never been any consensus about how F relates to its younger relation Q, nor about how either might be related to a supposed original manuscript.

The story which gained credence in the 1970s and 1980s was that Q might be based on the text of the play's first performance by the King's Men company for King James on Boxing Day evening 1606, and so is an authentic early version, but printed up from a scribbled draft difficult for the printer, probably an apprentice, to read (hence a lot of patent spelling mistakes), and that F is a separate version for later performance, possibly based on the acting company's prompt-book.

Many of Q's odder readings look like mere printing errors, for instance Lear casting off his *leadings* in Q which became his more comprehensible *lendings* in F (III.iv). In the same way, "to shoot/A troop of horse with felt" (mad

Lear in Q) makes no sense, but F's "to shoe/A troop of horse with felt" does (IV.vi). But there are many occasions where phrases and words in Q do make sense, but appear to have been deliberately and carefully changed in F.

Poor Tom's "Childe Rowland to the dark towne come" in Q, for example, even rhymes with the next line "His word was still 'Fie, foh and fum'", and any poet could easily have found that attractive; but it got changed to F's "Childe Rowland to the dark tower came" – more gothic and enigmatic and indeed arresting enough for Robert Browning to build around it one of his most enigmatic poems.

Sometimes the changes are small – "Nothing can come of nothing," says Lear to Cordelia in Q, which turns into "Nothing *will* come of nothing" in F (I.i). But other changes aren't. In Q, Goneril tells Edmund that she must change *armes* at home; in F she says she must change *names* (IV.ii). Which is a big difference: changing *arms* suggests swapping husband Albany's embraces for Edmund's; changing *names* suggests actually wanting to change husbands.

On plenty of occasions, small verbal changes make radically different, even quite opposite, meanings. In Q the Fool sneers at Kent that "Horses are tied by the heads"; but it's "by the heeles" in F (II.ii). If her sister is not "sick" (V.iii) Goneril will "ne'er trust medicine" in F; but "will ne'er trust poison'" in Q. In his Note for the Arden edition at this point, the editor R. A. Foakes nicely labels Goneril's medicine remark a sick joke; "stronger", he thinks, than the gibe about poison in Q, which is hardly a joke. But this is to miss the force of what's going on in these absolute differences between Q and F.

In oppositions such as *heads* and *heels,* and *poison* and *medicine,* meaning gets absolutely stuck, it's at an impasse, or *aporia* as the great French deconstructionist Jacques

Derrida labels such linguistic goings-nowhere.* And these poison-medicine type aporias are as it were the textual seasoning for *Lear*'s great accusatory satirical stew of allegations that there's no detectable difference between so many of the moral, philosophical and political opposites which the culture conventionally relies on: sight and blindness, reason and madness, judges and criminals.

There are, to be sure, various considerations apparently at work in F's changes. For instance, the invasion of the French on Cordelia's behalf in Q becomes an All-England civil war between Cordelia's force and the opposition in F: presumably because Shakespeare was nervous about any implication that an invasion by foreigners was a good thing. And some of F's large cuts look like the mere trimming of repetitious speeches, contradictory plot stuff and episodes not adding essentially to the fiction, in order to save on performance time.

But other F cuts, combining with some F additions, seem germane to the large purpose of making F an even grimmer play than Q. Notably, F eliminates from IV.i the couple of servants who in Q wish bad ends on Cornwall and Regan for blinding Gloucester, and who say they'll apply soothing "flax and whites of eggs" to Gloucester's "bleeding face", and get "the bedlam" Edgar to help the old Earl on his way.

F alters Albany a lot, especially minimising his fine humane revulsions. And it carefully endorses the play's gloomiest prognostications, as when Edgar offers the Beckettian imperative "Men must endure/Their going hence even as their coming hither./Ripeness is all", and F has Gloucester adding "And that's true too" (V.ii). In the F

*Arrestingly, one of Derrida's clearest examples of *aporia* is the *poison-medicine* one: Socrates in Plato's narrative having to commit suicide by drinking poison - *pharmakon* in Greek, which means simultaneously both medicine and poison.

version there's much enhancing of the play's negativities, sometimes quite literally so. In Lear's cry of intense despair over the body of the dead Cordelia – "And my poor fool is hanged" (V.iii) – F turns Q's two *nos* into three – 'No, no, no life", and tacks two extra *nevers* onto Q's three, which makes perhaps the most movingly bleak pentameter line in all of English literature:

> *Thou'lt come no more,*
> *Never, never, never, never, never.*

An intriguing exception to the heavy darkening of the ending by F are Lear's dying words in that version:

> *Do you see this? Look on her: look, her lips,*
> *Look there, look there!*

These words can be taken variously. Does Lear die happy, thinking Cordelia actually alive? Is this his final moment of delusion, of madness? Directors who want a really hope-less, utterly unconsoling play leave the lines out, as Peter Brook famously did in his momentously bleak 1962 RSC production.

Lear comes down to us heavily doctored, cleaned up, made legible in every way (old spelling and punctuation modernised for a start). Stage and film directors, of course, *have* to pick and choose, to settle and fix their *Lears*. Either Edgar or Albany has the play's last word; they can't both have it. Goneril can't trust both medicine *and* poison. Lear either says "nothing *will* come of nothing" or "nothing *can* come". And so on and on. But the reader can, and indeed should, entertain the play's numerous quite contrary possibilities – for they are intimately part of the play's rich, even tormenting, roster of oppositions and differences of meaning .

BIBLIOGRAPHY

The Textual Issues

Gabriel Egan, *The Struggle for Shakespeare's Text: Twentieth-century Editorial Theory and Practice* (Cambridge University Press, 2010).

TH Howard-Hill, 'The Two-Text Controversy', in *Lear from Study to Stage: Essays in Criticism*, edd James Ogden & Arthur H Scouten (associated University Presses, 1997), 31-41.

PWK Stone, *The Textual History of King Lear* (Scolar Press, 1980).

Gary Taylor & Michael Warren, *The Division of the Kingdoms: Shakespeare's Two Versions of King Lear* (Clarendon Press, 1983).

Steven Urkowitz, *Shakespeare's Revision of King Lear* (Princeton University Press, 1980).

Collections of Critical Essays

The Cambridge Companion to Shakespearian Tragedy, ed Claire McEachern (Cambridge University Press, 2002).

A Feminist Companion to Shakespeare, ed Dympna Callaghan (Blackwell, 2000).

Political Shakespeare: Essays in cultural materialism, edd Jonathan Dollimore & Alan Sinfield (Manchester University Press, 1985; expanded 1994).

Shakespeare's Tragedies, ed Emma Smith (Blackwell, 2004).

Critical & Critical-Historical Readings

Lynda E Boose, "The Father and the Bride in Shakespeare", PMLA (May 1982), 325-47.

Lynda E Boose, "The Father's House and the Daughter in It: The Structures of Western Culture's Daughter-Father Relationship", in *Daughters and Fathers*, edd Lynda E Boose & Betty S Flowers (Johns Hopkins University Press, 1989), 19-74.

AC Bradley, *Shakespearian Tragedy: Lectures on Hamlet, Othello, King Lear, Macbeth* (1904, 1905, etc).

Harold Bloom, *Shakespeare: The Invention of the Human* (Fourth Estate, 1999).

Stephen Booth, *King Lear, Macbeth, Indefinition, and Tragedy* (Yale University Press, 1983).

Stanley Cavell, "The Avoidance of Love: A Reading of King Lear", *Disowning Knowledge in Six Plays of Shakespeare* (Cambridge University Press, 1987), 39-123.

Ruby Cohn, "Lear Come Lately", *Modern Shakespeare Offshoots* (Princeton University Press, 1976), 232-266.

Brian Cox, *The Lear Diaries: the Story of the Royal National Theatre's Productions of Shakespeare's Richard III and King Lear* (Methuen, 1992).

John F Danby, *Shakespeare's Doctrine of Nature: A Study of King Lear* (Faber & Faber, 1961).

Jonathan Dollimore, *Religion, Ideology and Power in the Drama of Shakespeare and his Contemporaries* (Harvester Press, 1984).

Juliet Dusinberre, *Shakespeare and the Nature of Women* (Macmillan, 1975).

Margreta de Grazia, "The ideology of superfluous things: King Lear as period piece", in *Subject and object in Renaissance culture*, edd Margreta de Grazia, Maureen Quilligan, & Peter Stallybrass (Cambridge University Press, 1996), 17-42.

Michael Dobson, ed, *Performing Shakespeare's Tragedies Today: The Actor's Perspective* (Cambridge University Press, 2006).

William Empson, 'Fool in Lear', *The Structure of Complex Words* (Hogarth Press, 1985), 125-157.

DJ Enright, "King Lear and the Just Gods", *Shakespeare and the Students* (Chatto & Windus, 1970), 17-66.

Celeste Flower, *Shakespeare, King Lear: Cambridge Student*

Guide (Cambridge University Press, 2002).

RA Foakes, *Shakespeare and Violence* (Cambridge University Press, 2003).

SL Goldberg, *An Essay on King Lear* (Cambridge University Press, 1974).

Stephen Greenblatt, "Shakespeare and the Exorcists", *Shakespearian Negotiations: the Circulation of Social Energy in Renaissance England* (University of California Press and Clarendon Press, 1988), 94-128.

Samuel Johnson, "Preface" to his Edition of Shakespeare's Plays (1765), and its Notes on *King Lear*, in e.g. *Samuel Johnson on Shakespeare*, ed HR Woudhuysen (Penguin, 1989), 120-165, 219-223.

Coppélia Kahn, "The Absent Mother in King Lear", in *Rewriting the Renaissance: The Discourses of Sexual Difference in Early Modern Europe*, edd Margaret W Ferguson, Maureen Quilligan & Nancy J Vickers (University of Chicago Press, 1986).

David Scott Kastan, *Shakespeare After Theory* (Routledge, 1999).

G Wilson Knight, *The Wheel of Fire: Interpretations of Shakespearian Tragedy* (Oxford University Press, 1930; With Three New Essays, Methuen, 1954).

Jan Kott, *Shakespeare Our Contemporary*, translated Boleslaw Taborski, preface Peter Brook (Methuen, 1965; revised 1967).

Laurie E Maguire, *Studying Shakespeare: A Guide to the Plays* (Blackwell, 2004).

Tom McAlindon, "Cultural Materialism and the Ethics of Reading: or, the Radicalising of Jacobean Tragedy", *Shakespeare Minus "Theory"* (Ashgate, 2004), 87-104.

Colin McGinn, *Shakespeare's Philosophy: Discovering the Meaning Behind the Plays* (HarperCollins, 2006).

Steven Marx, "'Within a Foot of the Extreme Verge': the Book of Job and King Lear", *Shakespeare and the Bible* (Oxford University Press, 2000), 59-78.

Stephen Medcalf, "Dreaming, Looking, and Seeing: Shakespeare and a Myth of Resurrection", in *Thinking With Shakespeare, Comparative and Interdisciplinary Essays*, edd

William Poole & Richard Scholar (Legenda, 2007).

Dieter Mehl, *Shakespeare's Tragedies: An Introduction* (English translation, Cambridge University Press, 1986).

Kenneth Muir, *Shakespeare, King Lear*: Penguin Critical Studies (Penguin, 1986).

Carol Thomas Neely, "Reading the Language of Distraction: Hamlet, Macbeth, King Lear", *Distracted Subjects: Madness and Gender in Shakespeare and Early Modern Culture* (Cornell University Press, 2004), 46-68.

AD Nuttall, *Shakespeare the Thinker* (Yale University Press, 2007).

George Orwell, "Lear, Tolstoy and the Fool", Polemic no.7 (March 1947); *The Collected Essays, Journalism and Letters of George Orwell*, Vol 4, *In Front of Your Nose*, 1945-1950 (Penguin, 1970), 331-348.

Simon Palfrey, *Doing Shakespeare* (Arden, 2005).

Patricia Parker, "Preposterous Estates, Preposterous Events: From Late to Early Shakespeare", *Shakespeare from the Margins: Language, Culture, Context* (University of Chicago Press 1996), 20-55.

Carol Rutter, "Eel Pie and Ugly Sisters in *King Lear*", in *Lear from Study to Stage: Essays in Criticism*, edd James Ogden & Arthur Scouten (Associated University Presses, 1997), 172-225.

Carol Rutter, "Body Parts or Parts for Bodies: Speculating on Cordelia", *Enter the Body: Women and Representation on Shakespeare's Stage* (Routledge, 2001), 1-21.

Tony Tanner, "Introduction", *Shakespeare's Tragedies*, Vol 1 (Dent, 1992-3).

Leo Tolstoy, "Shakespeare and the Drama", *Tolstoy on Shakespeare*, translated V Tchertkoff (Free Age Press, 1907), 7-81; Oswald LeWinter, ed, *Shakespeare in Europe* (Penguin, 1970), 214-274.

Richard Wilson, *Secret Shakespeare: Studies in Theatre, Religion and Resistance* (Manchester University Press, 2004).

INDEX

A

Addison, Joseph 69
Albany, Goneril, turning against 38
Amis, Martin 105
Animal imagery 74-75, 80-81
Annesley, Brian 23
Anozie, Nonso 70
Aristotle, *Poetics* 107
Armin, Robert 42, 68
Asen, Abraham 113
Ashcroft, Peggy 39
Auden, W,H,
  "Musée des Beaux Arts" 117

B

Barber, Frances 91
Beckett, Samuel
  Breath 114
  Endgame 114, 115
  The Unnameable 118
  Waiting for Godot 67, 114-117
  Worstward Ho 117
Bennett, Alan
  The Madness of King George 71
Bergman, Ingmar 110
Bloom, Harold 75
  *Shakespeare and the Invention of
  the Human* 62, 110, 112
Boose, Lynda E.
  "The Father and the
  Bride in Shakespeare" 98
Booth, Stephen 35, 37
  "On the Greatness of
  King Lear" 107, 109
Bradley, A.C.
  *Shakespearian Tragedy:Lectures
  on Hamlet, Othello, King Lear,
  Macbeth* 5, 22-23, 27, 64-65
Breughel, Pieter 116-117
Brook, Peter 94, 113,
  114, 125

C

Catachresis 96

Catharsis 107
Cavell, Stanley 35
  *Disowning Knowledge; In
  Six Plays of Shakespeare* 74
Cohn, Ruby
  Modern Shakespeare Offshoots 117
Cordelia
  best portion, selected for 50
  Christian and forgiving
    nature of 50-53
  death of 4, 54, 57
  death, time of 119
  dutiful child, as 34
  flattery of Lear,
    refusing to give 37
  Lear turning against 24
  parodic marriage ceremony 100
  reunion with Lear 54
  unnatural behaviour 78-79
Cox, Brian 27

D

D-words 85-87
Derrida, Jacques 36, 86, 121, 124
Dollimore, Jonathan
  *Radical Tragedy: Religion,
  Ideology and Power in the
  Drama of Shakespeare and His
  Contemporaries* 54-56, 58
Donnelen, Declan 70
Dover Cliffs fraud 72-73, 88-89
Dusinberre, Juliet
  *Shakespeare and the
  Nature of Women* 95-98

E

Edgar
  baptism 62
  dutiful child, as 34
  importance of 61-67, 72-78
  manipulation of roles 72
  parallel Fool, as 64
  pretend letter from 90
  prig, as 74

religious character, as 76
self-abasement 64
shape-shifter, as 73
Stoicism 66, 72
Edmund
 malignity 79
 pretend letter from
 Edgar 90
 unnatural behaviour 36
Eliot, George 22
Elton, W.R. 105
Elyot, Sir Thomas
 The Boke of the Governor 31
Empson, William
 *The Structure of
 Complex Words* 53-54, 56
Enright, D.J. 74, 76
 Shakespeare and the Students 5-6
Epstein, Alvin 70
Ethical negativity 111

F
Foakes, R.A. 7, 26, 124
Fool 25, 41-45, 79, 83
Football, references in
 Shakespeare 71

G
Garai, Romola 47
Garnet, Father Henry,
 trial of 61
Geoffrey of Monmouth
 *History of the Kingdom
 of Britain* 22
Gielgud, John 39
Gloucester
 betrayals by 32-34
 blinding 4, 20, 34, 75, 102, 105
 insight, finding 20
 planetary influence,
  blaming bad things on 40
 speeches, lack of
  rationale or meaning 25
Gloucester Plot, origin of 20
Godard, Jean Luc 69
Gods, importance of 40-46
Goehr, Alexander

Promised End 110
Gokner, Cuneyt 70
Golan, Menaheim 69
Goneril
 Albany turning against 38
 intelligence and
  managerial skill 35
 mock-trial 43
Goold, Rupert 71
Grace, theological issue
 of 48-49
Greenblatt, Stephen
 Hamlet in Purgatory 58
 *Shakespearean
 Negotiations* 59-60
Greer, Germaine 77
Guinness, Alec 63

H
Halkin, Samuel 113
Handy-dandyism 27-28, 36, 45, 85
Harsnett, Samuel
 *A Declaration of
 Egregious Popishe
 Impostures* 19, 24-25, 59-60
Hawkes, Terence
 Writers and Their Work
 booklet 83
Hawthorne, Nigel 21
Hazlitt, William 69
Higgins, Henry
 Mirour for Magistrates 22
Hill, Christopher
 *The World Turned Upside
 Down* 83
Holinshed, Raphael
 *Chronicles of England,
 Scotland and Ireland* 22
Holy Communion 54-55
Host, use of term 36
Human animals 74-75
Hysteria 87, 94-97

J
James, Henry 26
Johnson, Dr Samuel 57, 69, 104
 Preface to Shakespeare 4

K

Kahn, Coppélia 94
  "The Absent Mother in
    King Lear" 101
Kent
  staunch servant, as 34
King Lear
  Arden text 26
  Beckett and the Theatre
    of the Absurd,
    looking forward to 112-122
  betrayals in 32-34
  breakdown in 29-40
  characters 6
  Christian themes and
    suggestions 46-58
  critics 25, 104-105
  darknesses of 19
  Double Plot 20
  ending 107-112
  film versions 69
  Freudianism in 100-101
  Gowthwaite Hall,
    performance at 61
  improbabilities and
    inconsistencies 23
  irresoluteness of 26-28
  language, undermining 85-92
  letters in 66-67
  madness of George III, banned during
71
  mutual obligation, breakdown of 30
  paralleled relationships 24
  plot, summary of 7-18
  previous stories, plundering of 18
  Quarto and Folio, versions of 122-126
  Roman Catholic and
    Protestant thrusts 58
  Shakespeare's lifetime,
    performance in 68
  Stationer's Register, in 31, 68
  subject matter of 18-28
  Tate's version 57, 69, 112, 124, 126
  text 7
  unanswered questions 27

  women, treatment of 92-107
  Yiddish translations 113
King Leir 19, 23
Knights, L.C. 26-27
Korol Lir 33
Kott, Jan 112-114

L

Lamb, Charles 26, 69
Language, undermining 85-92
Lawrence, D.H. 104
Lear (character)
  breakdown 29-40
  Cordelia, turning against 24
  dead Cordelia, carrying 52, 70, 109
  death of 19, 119-120
  division of kingdom 28
  Everyman in old age, as 110
  feminisation in
    referring to himself 86-87
  flesh, fascination by 101-102
  grace, gift of 49-50
  handy-dandy, game of
    27-28, 36, 85
  hostile weather around 80
  reunion with Cordelia 54
  speeches, lack of
    rationale or meaning 25
  Tom's advice to 73
  youngest and oldest actors playing 70
Leyr, King 18
Lustration 107
Lutheran Reformation 49

M

Macbeth
  predestination in 60
McAlindon, Tom
  *Shakespeare Minus
    "Theory"* 56
McCoy, Sylvester 99
McCready, Charles 69
McDonald, Russ 87
McKellan, Ian 69, 77
Measure for Measure 76

Medcalf, Stephen 52, 53, 61
Micoyels, Samuel 113
Middleton, Thomas
  The Revenger's Tragedy 111
Milton, John
  Samson Agonistes 107
Montaigne, Michel 55
Muir, Kenneth 60, 105

N
Nature, questioning of
  78-81
Ninagawa, Yukio 21
"Nothing", world reduced
  to 81-84
Novalis 22
Nuttall, A.D. 50, 52-53, 105

O
O'Brien, Geoffrey 88
Obligation, etymology of
  31-32
Olivier, Laurence 62
Orwell, George 25, 50, 53, 56, 104
Oswald 37, 65, 73
  insults thrown at 71

P
Palfrey, Simon 73
  Doing Shakespeare 66
Parker, Patricia 96-97
Power, segue into tyranny 109
Prayer Book, mutualities in 30-31
Precisians 76
Puttenham, George
  The Arte of English Poesie 97

R
Regan
  anatomising 103
  vileness of 35
Revelation, Book of 109
Rowe, Nicholas 70
Rutter, Carol 87, 93, 95-96
  Enter the Body 106

S
Salgado, Gamini
  *The Elizabethan
    Underworld* 83
Scapegoating 64
Sexual ranting 75
Shakespeare, William
  Catholic, whether 58
  mutual obligations,
    knowledge of 30-31
  women, treatment of 92-107
  sources 22-23
Sidney, Philip
  A Defense of Poesie 89
  Arcadia 20
Spenser, Edmund
  The Fairie Queene 22
Stubbes, Philip
  Anatomie of Abuses 88
Swinburne, Algernon
  Charles 104

Tate, Nahum
  King Lear, version of 45, 57, 69, 112
Theatre as agent of good 89
Tolstoy, Leo 24-25
Tom of Bedlam 44, 58-61
  rambling 85
Twelfth Night 76

Volchek, Galina 33

Wilson Knight, G.
  *The Wheel of Fire:
    Interpretations of
    Shakespearean Tragedy* 72
Wilson, Richard
  *Secret Shakespeare:
    studies in theatre,
    religion and
    resistance* 61
Women, treatment of 92-107
Woolf, Virginia
  A Room of One's Own 92-93

First published in 2012 by
Connell Guides
Spye Arch House
Spye Park
Lacock
Chippenham
Wiltshire SN15 2PR

10 9 8 7 6 5 4 3 2 1

Picture credits:
p.21 © Robbie Jack/ Corbis
p.33 © RIA Novosti/ Alamy
p.39 © Time Life Pictures/ Getty Images
p.47 © Geraint Lewis/ Alamy
p.63 © Everett Collection/ Rex Features
p.68 © Bolerat News/ Rex Features
p.77 © Geraint Lewis/ Alamy
p.91 © Geraint Lewis/ Alamy
p.99 © Geraint Lewis/ Alamy

A CIP catalogue record for this book is available from the British Library.
ISBN 978-1-907776-23-6

Design © Nathan Burton
Assistant Editor: Katie Sanderson
Printed in Great Britain by Butler Tanner & Dennis

www.connellguides.com